THE LIL' DEB'S OASIS COOKBOOK

PLEASE WAIT TO BE TASTED

JE 0 6 '22

Carla Kaya Perez-Gallardo, Hannah Black & Wheeler

PHOTOGRAPHY BY **Jessica Pettway**

FOREWORD BY **Meshell Ndegeocello**

PRINCETON ARCHITECTURAL PRESS · NEW YORK

This book is dedicated to all of our friends who had a hand in bringing this project to life; our incredible staff, who have dedicated countless hours of work and passion to keep us thriving; and every single person who has ever walked through our doors for a meal or a chat. Thank you. We wouldn't be here without you.

Published by
Princeton Architectural Press
70 West 36th Street
New York, NY 10018
www.papress.com

Editors: Abby Bussel, Sara Stemen
Designer: Natalie Snodgrass

For Lil' Deb's Oasis
Creative Direction: Lil' Deb's Oasis
Produced by Cousins
Producer: Anne Alexander
Food Styling: Victoria Granof
Prop Assistance: V. Haddad

Paintings on cover and pages i, ii–iii, vi–vii, 22–23, 48–49, 74–75, 124–25, 172–73, 226–27: Annie Bielski
Photograph on pages 20–21: Heidi's Bridge

Library of Congress Cataloging-in-Publication Data
—
Names: Perez-Gallardo, Carla Kaya, author. | Black, Hannah, author. | Wheeler, author. | Lil' Deb's Oasis (Restaurant)
Title: Please wait to be tasted : the Lil' Deb's Oasis cookbook / Carla Kaya Perez-Gallardo, Hannah Black, Wheeler; foreword by Meshell Ndegeocello.
Description: New York : Princeton Architectural Press, [2022] | Includes bibliographical references and index. | Summary: "Bold-flavored tropical comfort food fills this big-hearted celebration of food, love, and community-the first cookbook from Lil' Deb's Oasisin Hudson, New York"—Provided by publisher.
Identifiers: LCCN 2021042821 | ISBN 9781648960253 (hardcover)
Subjects: LCSH: Comfort food. | LCGFT: Cookbooks.
Classification: LCC TX714 .P4435 2022 | DDC 641.3—dc23
LC record available at https://lccn.loc.gov/2021042821

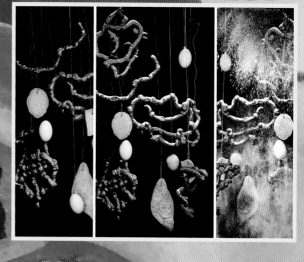

FOREWORD
BY MESHELL NDEGEOCELLO

We were in rehearsal for a live score of Ronald K. Brown's premiere of *Grace & Mercy* at Bard College, and we had grown tired of catered meals. I would pray for the rehearsals to run smoothly, so that I could hop in my car and return to Hudson without delay. After each session, I drove the thirty-five minutes for something that was rare and missed—a meal both nourishing and delicious. The food and feelings I pined for could only be had at Lil' Deb's Oasis.

I have lived in Hudson, New York, for many years, long enough to remember the sex workers on Union Street and the days when the work of local art hero Earl Swanigan could be acquired for trade. In January and February of those days, I could sometimes walk the full length of Warren Street, Hudson's main drag, in the middle of the street, without seeing another human being.

As a small city with a diverse population, Hudson is an unusual spot. Artists and queer folks started a creative migration from New York City in the 1980s, and the years since have brought huge changes. Flea markets have been replaced by fancy olive oil stores, some longtime residents and unusual characters have been displaced. But Hudson has also seen a new and committed generation of fighters: for equity in the economy, for small businesses, for new identities, for community fridges, for the astral travels of art and spirit and food and togetherness. Lil' Deb's Oasis respects in all directions, preserving what was here, while also creating something new. The building itself is exactly that—they kept the funny siding, they kept the name of the diner that previously occupied the space. But now, more than a restaurant or a style, it is a big movement in a tiny place.

Hudson has an excellent food scene, but for my palate it eventually became one-note. For those who crave salty, vinegary, spicy, colorful, warm Brown people food like yuca frita, sweet plantains, moqueca, and chicken soup that's not only delicious but also satisfying after a long day of work, there wasn't much. Since the day it landed, Lil' Deb's Oasis has been a paradise for me. The space itself is love-magic—bursting with color, light, beauty, and a sensual quality that was missing in our strange city. It feels like a declaration of truth, generosity, ferocious selfhood, and unapologetic fun. I am greeted without judgment and spoken to without assumptions. The music is always on point, and before I even eat anything, I feel a sense of nourishment and I remember that food is a portal to pleasure.

Sometimes I choose mojo chicken, served with hominy or aromatic rice. I often add an ensalada del dia, which is delicious enough that it can also be enjoyed as an entrée with a killer fresh tamale, perfectly proportioned with meat and masa. And because it is a true grub spot, I can order a fried egg atop any dish at Lil' Deb's Oasis.

Other times, I start my meal with a crudo. With husk cherries, capers, and fermented shiso leaves, it's plated like a bouquet, feeding the eye with bursts of color and joy. A salmon ceviche in bergamot agua delights me, and I love trying to discern each fantastic flavor. I can't resist the michelada, which never fails to transport me to the beach and feelings of sun.

But time after time, I find myself heading to Lil' Deb's Oasis for one thing only: the fried fish! It is fried to perfection in a gluten-free batter and placed upon a bed of strange herbs and greens. Where I grew up, fried fish loves a sauce—be it red hot sauce, tartar sauce, or pickled chiles—but this fried fish is served with a citrus-ginger sauce like no other. It is like a summer gravy, tangy from the fruit juice and ginger and held together by a floral olive oil that melts into the herbs and greens. This dish soothes the savage beast within me.

When dinner is over, I always opt for Abuela's Flan, made with the most loving hand, and topped with tiny flowers in honey. With its most perfect texture, this crème caramel makes me giggle like a child, and when I think about it from afar, I ache because I miss it so much.

I am the primary cook in my tribe and having a meal prepared by another can bring me to tears. During the summer of 2020, COVID-19 restrictions took their toll on the joy connectors, the folks who help you move past the shards and pricks of everyday life, the humans who make you sugar-free cocktails and bring you natural wines. Lil' Deb's Oasis took their magic to a tent with Fuego 69, creating an open-air experience and serving their Scallop and Jalapeño Skewers and Marinated Mushrooms, which are made with fermented carrots and scallion oil and combine soft and crunchy textures that give my lips that pleasant tingling sensation. I often found myself stopping at Fuego 69 for a quick snack after my daily walks and before heading home to start my own family's dinner.

Inside or outside, eating at Lil' Deb's makes my mind travel into the future even as I experience the now. It lets new life into my gray matter, and helps me to sort and discard memories, all while I'm lost in flavor. I leave the restaurant feeling connected and affirmed, alive and inspired. I remember why I love to cook.

It is a gift to be able to share the foods I love with the people I love, to eat so well that my whole body is grateful. I have called Lil' Deb's from my house to ask about the ingredients for a sauce or a spice in a dish. This cookbook, a guide to their mission, is what I've always wanted. Not everyone can create food that changes the mood of the individual and the air in the space. But now we can all try.

So, imagine you are in Hudson on your second day of antiquing, and while on your walk you come across a salmon-colored building. You walk in and you're greeted by beautiful faces, future celestial bodies, the feeling of naughty and nice. Welcome! You've entered an oasis indeed.

INTRODUCTION

WHAT IS TROPICAL COMFORT?

The story of Lil' Deb's Oasis began long before we knew who we were and who we wanted to be. It began when the restaurant was still a diner, twenty-six years before we even stepped foot inside the building, when the previous owner, Debbie Fiero, steered the ship of the eponymously named Debbie's Lil' Restaurant. She cooked up late-night meals for local firefighters, as well as 6:00 a.m. bacon and eggs for hungover teenagers. They came for the pancakes out of a box, but they also came for Debbie's huge smile and "help yourself" attitude: Her guests poured their own cups of coffee from the big percolator behind the counter. Debbie's Lil' Restaurant was a destination—for greasy spoon deliciousness and a warm welcome. And she *ran* the place, doing everything herself: cooking, serving, hosting, or offering "peel for a meal" trades with some of her regular guests. (If you ever want a free meal, just offer your time to the chef in charge, as there are always potatoes to peel or dishes to wash!) It was this openhearted spirit of tenacity, generosity, and resolve that we carried proudly with us as we began writing the chapters of our own mythology of what would become Lil' Deb's Oasis.

Though the colors and ambiance of the space quickly transformed when we signed the lease to our little 1,200-square-foot home in 2016, we knew we wanted to keep the essence of the restaurant's historical spirit and homespun hospitality. Marrying what Debbie had built with our own roller-coaster ride through flavor, color, experience, and sound was an opportunity we had been waiting for—a place to bring people together on our own terms, a place for everyone. After much-impassioned conversation, we realized that the food we wanted to make is best described as "tropical comfort food"—or, as we often say, "food that makes you sweat from places that make you sweat"—and that we wanted to serve it in an environment that brings people joy. We wanted to create a literal oasis of pleasure and community, with nourishment and connection as the central tenets.

The concept of the "tropics" is complicated. The word both defines and obscures, as it is often used interchangeably to describe anywhere sunny and beachy, often at the cost of acknowledging the rich and complex histories of the countries all over the world that make up "the tropics." Most of these places have faced colonization by European forces and other White supremacist empires. Many are still reeling from centuries of exploitation and displacement from their land, history, and identity. The very words that are often used to describe tropical regions—"warm," "exotic," and "welcoming"—also implicitly construct false consent, as if these varied cultures had invited the observation, infiltration, and subjugation by outside forces. These three words are colonial in essence, they frame the tropics as existing for the colonizer, slave-trader, and tourist.

The word "comfort" too is not devoid of classist and sometimes racist meanings. What does it mean when foods of cultures are described as "simple" and "comforting" within the context of Eurocentric haute cuisine? In American culture, comfort food is often associated with "soul food," a cuisine developed by creative Black cooks subjected to plantation slavery, Jim Crow, and persistent economic inequities. Comfort food is what your mother makes when there is nothing much in the pantry, or you are sick and in need of nourishment, but it is not often considered haute enough to be served at a fancy restaurant. In a hetero-patriarchal society, it often falls on women to provide comforting meals for their families at home, while white male chefs in white toques "elevate" the cuisine to be served with a high price tag. In contrast to preconceptions, comfort food is often not "simple" at all. It employs complex techniques and requires years of experience passed down through generations.

As we live among these contexts and attempt to reframe their narratives, "tropical comfort" has become a central ideal of our project. In this spirit, the term has become not only a description for the food we cook but also a way of understanding how we celebrate and hold complexity and dialogue as central to our mission, right alongside and intertwined with inclusion, generosity, deep connection, and a willingness to be proudly "other."

This framework also nods to the unconventional collision of our specific lineages. Hannah grew up in Alabama, eating ham-stuffed pork chops and fried catfish. On Sundays after church, her family lined up for country fried steak, collard greens, and cornbread served cafeteria-style at the real-life Whistle Stop Cafe, a classic "meat and three," where Fannie Flagg was inspired to write her novel *Fried Green Tomatoes*. Carla was raised in Queens, by an Ecuadorian mother obsessed with macrobiotic cooking and a grandmother who cooked professionally for Jewish families in New York. Her formative experiences of food were eclectic and layered by the gentle flavors central to macrobiotic vegetarian-Japanese fare, High Holiday meals like Rosh Hashanah celebrations, and the bright nourishment of traditional Ecuadorian foods, all interwoven with the threads of comfort and immigrant diaspora.

Ultimately, for us, "tropical comfort" best describes our sensibilities: hot, sticky, juicy, moist fever dreams of flavor; a genuine warmth and desire to share ourselves with you; and our penchant for adding unreasonable amounts of butter to our high-intensity lime-juicy, fish-saucy dishes. Comfort is what makes our restaurant feel like an oasis. It's in the colors, the lights, the music, and the food. It's in our irreverence for the traditional rules of restaurant ownership. And it's in the essence that is stained into our walls and hearts.

It's been six years since we opened our doors, yet we feel like a cat who's lived at least six of our nine lives. The joys! The lows! The lessons learned! The transformations! In many ways, our story is the story of *The Little Engine That Could*, the story of believing in something so fully that somehow—through will and testament and a genuine desire to feed, connect, and share the food we love—we would thrive. It's a story of romance and true love, of friendship and creative partnership, of supportiveness as lives shift and change, of facing life's scariest moments, hand-in-hand, ready to face the music. It's a story of faith.

This book is our way to bring our joy to your table at home: to share our love for pungent flavors; for piles of fresh herbs; and, most importantly, for gathering together around a big table that's full to the brim with plates of steaming food, brightly colored salads, and succulently fried fish, all perfect for eating with our fingers. It reveals the very instinctual, learning-by-doing approach we've taken with our food and space and is a how-to manual for throwing the best unintentional parties. It's a peek into our diaries, where we reveal our best-kept family secrets and tell you everything you wanted to know. Welcome to our world. We love having you here :)

Before we get too far, let's check in:

Part of what we've tried to offer at Lil' Deb's is a sort of iceberg freedom in a massaged kale world. It's not an irreverent offering—we mean no disrespect to a well-massaged, locally grown, hardy green salad! And we don't take for granted the blessed bounty of small farmers and farmworkers in the Hudson Valley, who have given us inspiration, camaraderie, and incredible food over the years.

But let's be real: We sling a lot of hot plantains, creamy avocados, and crispy iceberg lettuces at our restaurant here in the temperate Hudson Valley. These foods, our access to them, and so much else about our world, all bob in the wake of hundreds of years of colonization, dispossession, extraction, and the forced relocation of people, cultures, foods, and seeds. We have arrived here with a slate of tangible advantages in this system—fair skin, reliable health, and citizenship in this imperial and settler state, to name a few! If you're equipped with a similar slate, then this message is especially for you. Our job is to show up to this place with a combination of "humility and chutzpah."* Enough chutzpah to bear witness to a dizzying record of violence and trauma, and enough humility to keep our heads out of the sand, our hands in the work, and our hearts fed and full of solidarity.

Throughout this book, we'll try to share some of what we've learned as earnest students of the things we crave, though we make no claim to mastery and still look to other cooks, artists, and researchers for deep histories. But one point that we want to name, here and now, is that many of our ingredients and modes come from places embroiled in present-day struggles for food sovereignty—places reeling not just from the last five hundred years, but from the last fifty, thirty, ten years of neocolonialism, resource extraction, globalization, and agricultural imperialism. These processes are *ongoing*, the stuff of our lives and our neighbors' lives. These are the things that force people to leave and to carry their seeds with them.

We're not innocent. We're entangled, here in the ancestral territories of Lenni Lenape and Mohican peoples, on the banks of the river that runs both ways.

WRITTEN WITH SARA THOMAS BLACK

* to quote Southerners on New Ground, a multiracial, multigenerational organization for queer liberation in the Southern United States. See their resource "There Is Honor in Struggle, There Is Honor in the Work."

CHAPTER ONE

HOW TO FLIRT WITH THIS BOOK BECAUSE LEARNING IS SEXY

KITCHEN 101

elcome to our kitchen: It's hot and steamy here. Lush flavors bloom and recipes take unexpected twists and turns. Excitement and danger lurk behind every corner, your palms are sweaty, but you know you're ready—and you know you aren't alone. You belong here, with us, your trusty guides. We're here to welcome you in, shepherd you through, and teach you how to trust your instincts.

Your gut feelings are the most important tools you have, and to employ them well you must also tune in to your senses of sight, smell, sound, and, of course, taste. And taste, as you know, is subjective. We learn to trust our sense of taste through the experience of tasting, so we invite you to join us on this adventure—collapse with us into a mess of pleasurable sensations. This journey is about following your heart, learning to trust your hands and instincts, and figuring out what you enjoy through the lens of our hot and heavy recipe collection.

Our style of cooking, like good sex, requires a willingness to explore, play, and improvise. You can't take yourself too seriously, or you won't be able to have fun, so it's important to balance the desire to learn with a willingness to make mistakes and try again. If your instinct tells you to diverge from a particular recipe instruction, we encourage you to follow your own lead, to play with ingredients, flavors, and yourself. At the end of the day, it's you who will decide what tastes good (aka what feels good), and trusting where you will land also comes through experience and thoughtful repetition. Cooking is an exercise in the production of pleasure—the more you do it, the easier it becomes to recognize the path to getting there. The more comfortable you are with the process, the easier it will be to stop and smell the roses you will undoubtedly find along the way. And the more you play and explore, the deeper and more gratifying the final payoff becomes.

At this point, you're probably starting to pick up what we're putting down. Yes, we're flirting with you! And we'd love you to flirt back. This chapter begins a mutual exploration of how we can best flirt together to create unforgettable experiences and lasting memories ;)

"Is it hot? Does it look good? Are you proud to serve it?" This phrase may come from a meme about how to send nudes, but it's also a cheeky mantra that we live by. These are the kinds of questions we've asked ourselves and our kitchen team over the years. They outline the framework we apply to every dish: Is the dish the ideal temperature for serving? Is it presented as thoughtfully and beautifully as possible? Are you proud of the work you're putting out? Does it represent your best effort and intention? If the answer to any of these questions is no, we ask our staff to consider what they can do to move the dish toward a pleasure zone of awe and excitement. We hope you can begin to ask yourself these questions as you work through our recipes and establish your own framework for what looks, feels, and tastes good to you. Within these questions lie subsets of important information that are equally vital to building your own framework:

Color

What is the color story of a dish? Sometimes we like to lean into a monochrome style of food presentation, but for the most part, we like to make food that represents nature's vast spectrum of colors. This isn't only for aesthetic reasons. Thinking about color pushes us to consider the flavors that are experienced within the color spectrum. Color has psychological effects, and it can even impact how we perceive flavor and experience taste.

For example, red-colored foods—like chile peppers and red onions, paprika and tomatoes—are often packed with flavors associated with spice, heat, and intensity. White-colored foods—like scallops, rice, and cream of wheat—tend to be associated with subtle flavors and sometimes even blandness. Obviously, these aren't hard-and-fast rules, but they do speak to the ways that color is vital to our understanding of flavor. For us, no one color has one association; we paint indiscriminately with nature's bountiful palette.

Texture

We're often looking for a variety and contrast of textures in each dish: Does this ceviche or salad contain elements that are chewy, creamy, firm, or crispy? Most often, we gravitate toward dishes that contain at least three of these elements, but sometimes (like in our Scallop Crudo with Green Banana, Coconut, and Dill, page 95) we prefer to focus more on overlapping textures that lead to an enjoyable confusion of the palate. In many of our dishes, we often add a generous sprinkle of a seed or nut to add a crunchy texture to something otherwise soft or creamy. As you cook with us, you'll learn how to make these kinds of informed decisions.

Flavor

One of our greatest pleasures at the restaurant is when we start to clear a table and a customer yells, "Wait! Stop! We want to keep it for the sauce!" Our sauces are meant to layer on top of one another and meld together in one big mouth orgy of flavor. Some of our best dishes have one sauce, while others have two or even three. (Oftentimes, our guests will take matters into their own hands, merging sauces from different dishes to create their own experience.) This harmonic abundance of sauces, layered with handfuls of herbs, juicy pickles, and spice dusts, makes your tongue pulse and your belly smile.

If there's a secret to our food, it is the concept of more. More herbs! More salt! More acid! More spice! We challenge our cooks to get to know the edge of flavor, to get comfortable with it, and we encourage you to do the same. How close to the edge can you get without falling off the cliff? Of course, not every dish needs to be packed with a punch, but most of our food is a loose, wild balance of acid, spice, and salt. If you taste something and find that it isn't quite "there" yet, it most likely needs more of one of those three elements. As you cook, imagine that we're whispering "more! more! more!" into your ear until you take your sauce right to the edge—and no further.

All the best recipes are built on layers of flavor. If you think about a dish from the inside out or the bottom up, and always remember to season accordingly, you're going to get amazing results. If you're boiling water to cook pasta, it needs salt! The ceviche agua you're creating from a mélange of summer fruit? It needs both acid and salt! Make your vinaigrettes robust, bright, and briny! And don't forget your finishing salt! Basically, you want flavor *everywhere*. But you also need to learn when to stop, when to hold back, when to let an ingredient shine.

Again, much like sex, this process requires building trust. We hope the recipes in these pages will empower you to trust your palate, build relationships with your ingredients, combine flavors that might sound freaky together, and heed the call for "more! more! more!" You'll end up sighing from maximal contentment and pleasure.

Maybe you're ready to take the dive with us or maybe you're still nervous. Since we're all consenting adults, here are a few simple guidelines for making your way through this book:

1. TASTE AS YOU GO. To cook well, you need to understand how to build flavor, and tasting is an essential part of the process. Keep a collection of your favorite small spoons on hand. Use them to taste the dish throughout the cooking process—after you've added the first layer of seasoning, while you're cooking or marinating, and right before you serve it. Doing so gives you access to the rapidly shifting world of flavors—the way they bloom when left to sit, or the way they are absorbed to reveal the need for more of an ingredient to make a dish complete. Over time, you'll be able to interpret the information being shared with you by the ingredients themselves.

2. LEARN TO LOVE MISE EN PLACE. While our restaurant is decidedly not modeled on the French brigade system, mise en place is a most important lesson and tool for working. The phrase means "everything in its place," which is an essential tenet of the art of cooking. At its core, this means being prepared ahead of time—make your shopping list, gather your ingredients, clean your space, and set up your workstation. It means cut your vegetables before you start to cook, season your meat the night before, have your sauces ready and your knives sharpened. Mise en place gives you the freedom to play, experiment, and get weird.

3. EAT WITH YOUR HANDS! Your fingers are your first points of contact—your receptors of texture and temperature. Natural neural pathways to flavor and pleasure are stymied without the sense of touch. Forks and knives are important tools but not more important than your hands. Many cultures cook and eat with their digits, and it is our belief that everyone should. It furthers your intimacy with and connection to your food. In our wildest dreams, this would occur from the planting of seeds in rich, dark soil through harvesting and washing, preparation, and cooking, and finally to consumption. We must remember the labor of all the hardworking hands that have touched our food with love long before it hits our table. After all, many hands have tended the foods we eat, from the field to the farmers' market or grocery store. Use your hands, and don't be afraid to get messy—it's a part of experiencing joy!

4. COOK WITH COMPANY. We believe that sustenance is a communal responsibility, and no one should have to go it alone. Most of our recipes are designed for larger gatherings, and though they work equally well for the solo cook, we encourage you to cook in community. While we know the pleasure of a night spent cooking solo in the kitchen with your favorite music on, we encourage you to work in tandem with a trusted and open-minded friend or perhaps a lover. This will both lighten your workload and amplify your experience of eating, because pleasure designed for multiplicity is often greater than pleasure designed for one. (For more thoughts on dining together, see our "Soft Rules" on page 177.)

5. MAKE OUR FRAGRANT CHILE OIL (PAGE 38) BEFORE YOU DO ANYTHING ELSE. Not only because we recommend adding some as a final garnish to most of our dishes, but also because you'll want to add it to everything you already make at home, from your morning egg scramble to your favorite chocolate dessert.

6. PLAN AHEAD. Many of our recipes call out processes that are meant to be done ahead of time—to improve the final flavor of a dish as well as streamline its preparation and make it less stressful.

7. DON'T BE AFRAID TO IMPROVISE! Some of our ingredients are seasonal, regionally specific, or sourced at specialty stores. Feel free to tweak our recipes to suit your tastes and fancies, and take advantage of what's in your fridge or available where you live. Sometimes the best way to get creative is to work within the constraints at hand. Most of our recipes provide guidelines for making substitutions, but don't be afraid to take risks. And if it doesn't work out, don't cry! Try again. Remember to have fun, play around, loosen your grip, take a breath, and dig in!

Fantasy Pantry

It's always good to be prepared before launching into a new experience. Here's a list of the most essential ingredients to have on hand—for everyday cooking or to spice things up on the fly.

ACIDS
* black vinegar
* Chile Vinegar (page 39)
* distilled vinegar
* freshly squeezed lemon juice
* freshly squeezed lime juice
* freshly squeezed orange juice
* red wine vinegar
* rice vinegar
* umeboshi vinegar
* white wine vinegar

FLOURS
* all-purpose flour
* buckwheat flour
* cornstarch
* rice flour
* tapioca starch

OILS
* canola oil
* coconut oil
* extra-virgin olive oil
* Fragrant Chile Oil (page 38)
* herb oil

SEASONINGS
(If it's an option, buy whole and toast or grind as needed.)
* Aleppo pepper
* allspice berries
* annatto seeds
* black peppercorns
* Chile Dust (page 37)
* cloves
* coriander seeds
* cumin seeds

* dried chiles (amarillo, ancho, árbol, guajillo)
* fennel seeds
* garlic powder
* ground turmeric
* Mole Powder (page 36)
* pink peppercorns
* smoked paprika
* star anise pods
* sumac
* sweet paprika
* Szechuan peppercorns
* Tajín
* urfa biber (an all-time fave for its smoky, earthy, tangy flavor)
* white peppercorns
* yellow mustard seeds

SWEETENERS
* buckwheat and other honeys
* granulated sugar
* maple syrup
* palm sugar

UMAMI
* anchovies
* capers
* cotija cheese
* dried mushrooms
* dried shrimp
* fish sauce
* nori/dried seaweed
* nutritional yeast
* Parmesan cheese
* soy sauce or tamari

Toolbox

Flip, Scrape, and Spread

FISH SPATULA: Named for its prowess in gently lifting fish from a pan without tearing its delicate skin, this slotted version of a metal spatula also drains off oils as you flip.

METAL SPATULA: All you need to flip that hot thing real quick! Good for scraping those crispy bits off the pan! Just don't use it on nonstick surfaces.

OFFSET SPATULA: Used for frosting cakes or slicing flan.

RUBBER SPATULA: We hate wasting sauces (we told you we are sauce-crazy) and these babies help you scrape every bit off the side of your bowl or blender. A high-heat version is great for working with caramel or stirring in a nonstick pan.

Grate and Peel

MANDOLINE: No other tool allows you to easily create thin, even slices of fruits and vegetables, and the additional blade attachments come in handy when you want to julienne a carrot or radish. Please keep your eyes on your delicate fingers, as a mandoline's sharp blades can cause serious damage to your digits if not handled properly.

MICROPLANE: If you don't already have one, you must buy one! We use them for everything—finely zesting citrus, easily grating garlic and ginger, or quickly creating pillows of feathery cheese.

Y-PEELER/SWISS PEELER: The wide handle makes it easy to remove skin from citrus or peel an apple in one straight shot. They are double-bladed, making them easy for both lefties and righties to use. They also come in cute colors, and who doesn't love that in a kitchen?

Juice and Grind

BLENDER: If you don't have one, we highly recommend making an investment before you get too deep into our recipes. We are a sauce-lovin' family, with a need for speed, so a good high-speed blender is a worthwhile investment. You'll need one to achieve smooth, bright-colored sauces, but it's also perfect for a quick morning smoothie (page 54), so you can't go wrong.

CITRUS JUICER: You can squeeze juice out of citrus with your hands, but we LOVE acid way too much to lose even a single drop. We use an electric version at the restaurant, because we go through a lot of juice, but you'll do just fine with a simple hand juicer or reamer.

FOOD PROCESSOR: This modern version of the mortar and pestle is ideal for making aioli, creating pastes and nut butters, and quickly blitzing herbs, vegetables, and seeds.

MORTAR AND PESTLE: Essential to human survival for the preparation of medicine, cosmetics, and food as far back as 35,000 BCE, the mortar and pestle is the original food processor and can be used for both dry and wet ingredients. While it requires time and patience that some home cooks may not possess, we love using this ancient technique to pound spices and make sauces, as it produces incomparable texture and flavor.

Measure and Pour

MEASURING CUP: We must admit that we rarely use these because exact measurements aren't our thing, but we'll be honest and say we love the pour spout on liquid measuring cups because they make it easy to pour soup and other liquids into bowls and storage containers.

MEASURING SPOONS: We feel the same way about measuring spoons as we do measuring cups, but they are helpful when you want to be precise :)

Slice and Chop

PARING KNIFE: Perfect for small tasks like preparing citrus supremes, deveining shrimp, and cutting smaller fruits and vegetables.

CHEF'S KNIFE: A kitchen essential, this versatile knife is great for cutting vegetables and meat, preparing herbs using the chiffonade technique, and chopping nuts. Just keep her sharp and watch your fingers!

CLEAVER: Best for splitting meat from the bone, cutting larger vegetables like squash, or working your way through harder shelled crustaceans like lobster.

Whip, Stir, and Taste

CHEF'S SPOON: Larger than a soup spoon, this is necessary for swooshing and schmearing sauces on plates.

SPIDER/SLOTTED SPOON: Essential for any fry job, spiders and slotted spoons allow you to safely lift things out of hot liquids.

TASTING SPOONS: Never forget to taste! We like to collect special spoons for this purpose—start building your collection of this essential tool.

WOODEN SPOON: Great for stirring and scraping up crispy bits from the bottom of a pan without scratching it, which is especially important with delicate surfaces like nonstick pans. Get yourself a wooden spoon you love and treat her well. We like to have them in different sizes.

WHISK: Great for easily incorporating ingredients and breathing extra air into sauces when whipping them into shape.

TONGS: Can't live without them! Flip, lift, and turn with ease. Once you get used to them, these gals start to feel like extensions of your own hand. Also: tongs make great impromptu castanets when you're cooking and your favorite song comes on :)

Spice Mix Recipes

We turn to our homemade spice mixes whenever we want to build flavor from the bottom up, which is pretty much always. They are great to keep on hand for easy dinnertime seasoning, plus they are shelf-stable. You can make your own seasoning salts using any spices, herbs, or dried flowers you like, but here's a peek into some of our pantry favorites:

LEMON VERBENA SALT

Yields 2½ cups

1½ oz dried lemon
   verbena leaves
2½ cups kosher salt

We love when fresh lemon verbena comes into season in the Hudson Valley. We buy up a bunch from our local farms and use it in cocktails, desserts, and salads. Its sweet lemony scent makes a beautiful tea when steeped in hot water. What we don't use immediately, we dry out to preserve for lemon verbena salt, so that we can enjoy the flavor all year long, and we encourage you to do the same if you find fresh lemon verbena at the market. Otherwise, dried leaves are easily ordered online. This salt is a great seasoning on fish, lamb, chicken, or fresh fruit, but feel free to experiment and substitute in lieu of regular salt, for any dish that is crying for a little herbaceous kick.

In a high-speed blender, blend the lemon verbena into a fine powder—it should yield about 1½ cups. Pour into a bowl, picking out and discarding any stray stems. Add the salt and mix together. Store in an airtight container for up to a year.

MAGIC DUST

Yields 1 cup

3 Tbsp allspice berries
2 Tbsp coriander seeds
2 Tbsp yellow mustard
   seeds
1 Tbsp black peppercorns
1 Tbsp cumin seeds
1 Tbsp fennel seeds
1 tsp cloves
20 cardamom pods
5 star anise pods
1 cinnamon stick

At the restaurant, we call this seasoning dust "Fish XXX," because it's what we sprinkle on our whole fried fish after frying. But it's not a one-trick pony made only for fish, so for this book, we are calling it "magic dust." It really is a magical combination of warming spices in the same vein as Chinese five-spice powder. Try it with lamb, in a chocolate-based dessert, or on popcorn!

In a large pan over low heat, toast the allspice, coriander, mustard, peppercorns, cumin, fennel, cloves, cardamom, star anise, and cinnamon, stirring, until fragrant, about 6 minutes. Allow to cool slightly, then transfer to a spice grinder or high-speed blender and grind into a fine powder. Store in an airtight container at room temperature for up to a year.

LEMON VERBENA XXX

MAGIC DUST

MOLE POWDER

MOLE POWDER

Yields 1 cup

¼ cup ground sumac

4 tsp unsweetened cacao powder (substitute with unsweetened cocoa powder)

1 Tbsp coriander seeds

1 Tbsp cumin seeds

1 Tbsp yellow mustard seeds

1½ tsp cloves

1¼ tsp ground cinnamon

1 tsp ground allspice

1 tsp ground coffee

5 star anise pods

4 dried chiles de árbol or 2 tsp crushed red pepper flakes

2 dried guajillo chiles, seeds removed

3 Tbsp toasted sesame seeds

A balance of sweet, heat, a little bitterness, and rich nuttiness—sounds like a metaphor for life—the flavor profile for this spice mixture draws inspiration from Mexico's beautifully complex sauce. We only use classic mole dry ingredients and have taken a few liberties based on what we keep in our pantry. Use this powder with our Blistered Peppers with Mole Powder (page 87), to season chicken, beef, or even roasted squash, or to add some heat to your favorite dessert.

In a large pan over low heat, toast the sumac, cacao powder, coriander, cumin, mustard, cloves, cinnamon, allspice, coffee, star anise, chiles de árbol, and guajillo chiles, stirring, until fragrant, 4 to 6 minutes. Allow to cool slightly, then transfer to a spice grinder and grind into a fine powder. Stir in the sesame seeds. Store in an airtight container at room temperature for up to a year.

CHILE DUST

Yields ½ cup

2 Tbsp Tajín
2 Tbsp sweet paprika
2 Tbsp sumac
2 Tbsp Aleppo pepper
2 tsp cayenne pepper
2 tsp kosher salt

Tajín is a delicious Mexican seasoning consisting of chili powder, salt, and dehydrated lime. It's used all over the world and is perfect for adding some heat and tang to chips or fresh fruit, or as a rim for a delicious margarita or michelada. We combine Tajín with a few of our pantry favorites and use it for sprinkling on our Salchipapas Bravas (page 140), roasted potatoes, and chips of all kinds.

Mix all ingredients together and love your life. Store in an airtight container for up to 6 months.

CRISPY GARLIC CHIPS

Yields ½ cup

10 garlic cloves, peeled
6 cups whole milk or water
2 cups canola oil

Why is this process so involved? Good question! Blanching the garlic in milk (or water, if you prefer) helps to mellow its intensity and reduce the potential for acrid flavor. We think it is deeply worth the effort.

On a mandoline, shave the garlic lengthwise. The slices should be thin but not translucent. In a small pot, bring the shaved garlic and milk to a boil. Drain the garlic through a strainer and discard the liquid. Repeat this process two more times, for a total of three boils and drains. After the final drain, put the garlic on paper towels.

In a small pot over low heat, combine the blanched garlic and canola oil. Heat until bubbles of water released from the garlic begin to appear at the surface of the oil. (These bubbles are water that is being released from the garlic, and they are the single most important element to guide you.) Continue heating until the bubbles stop appearing and the garlic is crispy and golden, about 30 seconds. Immediately remove the garlic and drain on fresh paper towels. Season with salt. Store the garlic chips in an airtight container at room temperature for up to 2 weeks; refrigerate the oil in an airtight container for up to 2 months. Reuse the oil to make more garlic chips, prepare garlic confit, drizzle on bread, use in vinaigrettes, or toss with vegetables before roasting.

Spice of Life!

We like to use a lot of heat in our cooking. Not that everything is super spicy, but nearly all our dishes get a dash of heat in some form or another. The fun thing about adding spice to your food at home is that it's up to you how much or how little you want to add! Below are some of our classic turn ups, so you can pop it like it's hot from the comfort of your own home.

FRAGRANT CHILE OIL

Yields 1 quart

2 Tbsp annatto seed (optional, but really intensifies the desired bold red color)

20 dried chiles de árbol (for spice)

5 dried chipotle or morita chiles (for smoke)

5 dried guajillo chiles

6 dried pulla (puya) chiles

3 star anise pods

1 garlic head, halved crosswise

1 cinnamon stick

1 qt canola or other neutral oil

We put our chile oil on EVERYTHING. It adds a beautiful bold red color and pleasant heat that perfectly finishes any dish. At this point, we can't eat anything without it, but maybe that's just us :) Keep both the oil and the ground chile "sludge," which can be used to add warm heat and depth of flavor to pretty much anything you can think of, from vinaigrettes to braises, as well as the Cacao-Buckwheat Chile Crisp that complements our S'mores 69 (page 245). The red chile oil can be used religiously on everything you eat! Note that the chiles and garlic will continue to cook after you take them off the heat, so make sure to pay attention to when they begin floating—if you wait longer, they'll likely start to burn.

In an 8 qt stockpot, combine the annatto seeds, chiles de árbol, chipotle or morita chiles, guajilla and pulla chiles, star anise, garlic, and cinnamon. Add the oil and bring to a simmer over low heat. Continue gently simmering until the chiles are plump and float to the top and the garlic begins to take on a golden hue, about 5 minutes. Turn off the heat and allow the oil to cool.

Working in batches, blend the cooled oil mixture in a blender on high until all the chiles and spices are pulverized. Pour through a fine-mesh sieve, reserving both the oil and the solids. Store the oil in an airtight container at room temperature for up to 1 month; store the ground chile "sludge" in an airtight container and refrigerate for up to 2 months.

CHILE VINEGAR

Yields 1½ quarts

16 dried chiles de árbol,
 stems removed
5 dried guajillo chiles,
 stems removed
1½ qt distilled white vinegar

This chile vinegar is bright, beautiful, and so easy to make. We highly recommend dashing some on breakfast potatoes, any cabbage dish, or to quickly spice up a vinaigrette!

In a medium pot, bring the chiles de árbol, guajillo chiles, and vinegar to a boil over high heat. Turn the heat to low and simmer until the chiles have softened, about 5 minutes. Turn off the heat, cover, and let stand for 30 minutes. Remove the lid and allow to cool slightly.

Working in batches, blend the cooled vinegar mixture in a blender on high until it turns red and becomes homogeneous. Pour into a qt sized bottle or old wine bottle and refrigerate up to 6 months.

HOT SAUCE

Yields 1½ quarts

¼ cup granulated sugar
3 Tbsp kosher salt
1 Tbsp allspice berries
1 tsp cloves
10 dried chiles de árbol
5 dried ancho chiles
5 dried guajillo chiles
5 garlic cloves
4 star anise pods
1 qt distilled white vinegar

Our house hot sauce is the perfect balance of deep, rich, warming spices (cloves, star anise, and allspice), sweet and bright sugar and vinegar, and, of course, the hot heat of our blend of chiles. Enjoy with eggs, rice, fruit, chips, or anything that needs a little extra zing!

In a medium pot, bring the sugar, salt, allspice, cloves, chiles de árbol, ancho chiles, guajillo chiles, garlic, star anise, vinegar, and 2 cups of water to a boil over high heat. Turn the heat to low and simmer until the chiles puff up, the spices are infused, and the sugar melts, about 20 minutes. Turn off the heat and allow to cool completely.

Working in batches, blend the mixture in a blender on high until completely smooth. This process may take up to 10 minutes or more, as the whole spices take a while to break down, and you may need to let your blender rest, so it doesn't overheat. Season with salt as you like—hot sauce should be spicy, tangy, and a tiny bit sweet. Pour through a fine-mesh sieve and discard any solids. Store the hot sauce in an airtight container in the refrigerator for up to 3 months.

Pickling

We love pickles! We put them on EVERYTHING! Almost any dish can be heightened with the exquisitely briny flavor and bold magenta color of pickled red onions, but many other fruits and vegetables are calling out to be pickled too! We typically use one of three types of picking methods: citrus quick pickles, vinegar brines, and lacto-fermentation. Each one requires a different process and therefore yields distinct results!

Citrus, or "quick," pickles are the fastest, on-the-fly way to add a little brightness to any dish. Throw some lime juice on some sliced red onion and you're halfway to flavor-bomb heaven. However, the shelf-life of citrus pickles is much shorter, only a day or so, than that of vinegar or lacto-fermented pickles.

With vinegar pickles, you have the option of hot or cold brines, which impacts the texture, and often the color, of your finished pickles. Cold brines tend to allow the fruit or vegetable you are pickling to retain its original color, while hot brines often soften the texture of your pickles much more and also change their color! We like to use a hot brine with our pickled red onions, for example, because the heat tends to bring out a brighter pink color than a cold brine, but their final color often depends on things you can't control, such as the age of the onions you're using.

Lacto-fermentation is achieved by creating an environment where lactic acid can safely thrive, by using salt, whey, or starter cultures like Japanese koji. Our recipes focus on salt-based lacto-ferments, as they are simple and a great place to begin your relationship with pickle-making.

We aren't here to tell you the science behind how lacto-fermentation works. A quick Google will give you that information from far more knowledgeable sources, but we can tell you that you should be lacto-fermenting everything. Have fun and experiment! The more you do it, the less intimidating the process feels because you'll start to recognize the different stages of the pickle as it ferments and begin to intuit when it's "ready" by following its fermentation journey as it develops that good funky smell.

With pickle making, there is so much room to play around with the flavors and seasoning. You can customize our pickling brine to suit your preferences, substituting your favorite spices to create different flavor combinations.

Below is a non-exhaustive list of fruits and vegetables for pickling in no particular order:

red or white onions	**chiles**	**cauliflower**
tomatoes	**cucumber**	**garlic**
tomatillos	**carrots**	**turnip greens**
apples	**radishes**	**mushrooms**
pineapple	**mustard greens**	
	cabbage	

QUICK CITRUS PICKLE

Yield depends on ingredient selection

1 shallot or red onion or white onion or whatever you're trying to pickle on the fly
Juice of 2 lemons or limes
2 tsp kosher salt

Slice your vegetable of choice nice and thin or shave it on a mandoline. Cover in enough lemon or lime juice to thoroughly coat your ingredient and stir in the salt. Allow to marinate for 20 to 30 minutes before serving.

VINEGAR PICKLE

Yields 1½ quarts brine

This is the standard spice combination we use at the restaurant, but feel free to experiment, as there are a plethora of herbs and spices you could use— think dill, turmeric, garlic, oregano, and caraway.

2 cups granulated sugar
1 cup kosher salt
1 Tbsp allspice berries
1 Tbsp cloves
1 Tbsp star anise pods
1 Tbsp cardamom pods
1 orange, halved
1 qt white distilled vinegar, white wine vinegar, or apple cider vinegar

This recipe will work with about one pound of any fruit or vegetable, but we most often use this brine to make our pickled onions, chiles, and pineapple. How you cut the veggies is up to you, just keep in mind that the size of the cut will impact how long it takes the pickle brine to fully penetrate, preserve, and flavor your veggie of choice. For example, onions that are thinly shaved on a mandoline can be ready to use the same day they are pickled. The same goes for pickled pineapple if you cut the pineapple into ¼ inch pieces and chiles (we love using Fresnos) if you slice them into rounds about ⅛ inch thick. A heartier vegetable like turnip or carrot may take longer to pickle, so we recommend storing those for at least 24 to 48 hours in the brine before serving.

In a stockpot, bring the sugar, salt, allspice, cloves, star anise, cardamom, orange, vinegar, and 2 cups of water to a boil over high heat. Boil until the sugar and salt dissolve and the spices infuse, about 5 minutes. Turn off the heat. (We like hot brine for onions and chiles and cool brine for pineapple, but cool will work for everything.) Pour through a fine-mesh sieve and discard the solids. Place your cut veggies into qt sized glass jars, pour the brine over the cut vegetables, and refrigerate overnight before serving. Store in an airtight container in the refrigerator for up to 2 months.

Lacto-Fermented Pickles

We love the funky, briny, sparkly taste that lacto-fermentation brings to a pickle. The process preserves and heightens flavors, textures, and nutrients. Plus, it gives food that extra umami complexity. The more you do it, the less intimidating the process will feel. As you start to recognize the different stages of the pickle as it ferments, you will begin to intuit when it's "ready" by experiencing its fermentation journey as it develops that good funky smell.

Salt is a preservative, and it truly honors and amplifies the flavors of the ingredients it binds with, bringing out their subtle complexities and allowing their magical flavors to sing. We use a 3 percent brine solution for most of our lacto-fermented pickles. This means that you'll need to know the weight of the item you're pickling, and then do a little math to figure out how much salt to use, so this is one of the rare times we'll ask you to use a kitchen scale for accuracy. For this example, let's use carrots!

LACTO-FERMENTED CARROTS

Yield depends on the amount of carrots used

Carrots
Filtered, non-chlorinated
    water
Kosher salt
Whole peeled garlic

This recipe is offered as a technique with ratios as parameters and can be adapted to work with any amount of product. Consider using chiles, radish, turnip greens, or any other favorite vegetable.

Peel your carrots and leave them whole or cut them into matchsticks, rounds, or any style you prefer—the larger the vegetable, the longer it may take to ferment.

Find a vessel that fits your carrots, with a little room at the top to cover with brine. Using a kitchen scale, tare the vessel you are using (weigh it empty and deduct its weight from the total weight of vessel and water), and fill it up a little more than halfway with filtered water—you want the weight of the water in grams or ounces. Multiply the weight of the water times 0.03—the amount of kosher salt you want to use.

Transfer the water to a pot. Measure the salt and add it to the pot. Bring to a boil over high heat and boil until the salt has dissolved. Turn off the heat and cool to room temperature.

Meanwhile, arrange the carrots and garlic in the vessel. Once the brine is at room temperature, pour it over the carrots, making sure they are fully submerged in the liquid. It's helpful to use a weight, like a small plate or bowl, to keep the carrots from floating up as they ferment. Lay plastic wrap over the surface of the liquid and then over the vessel before setting the weight on top.

Loosely cover the vessel with a lid, set in a tray or baking dish or on kitchen cloth (in case it starts to bubble), and place in a warm, dark place to ferment, checking on them regularly to see how they're progressing! After 3 days, check the carrots for your desired level of crunch, tang, fizz, and funk. Is it there yet? If not, let it sit for another day or so. When ready, cap the lid and refrigerate to halt the fermentation process. Store the pickles in the refrigerator for up to 6 months.

A Note on Mold

During the fermentation process, you might notice a white film form on top of your brine. Don't be discouraged. This is kahm yeast, which is normal and natural, so simply scrape it off with a spoon or fine-mesh spider. If you notice pink, red, or black mold, or a slimy quality to the brine, then your batch has spoiled. This is rare, so don't stress, just follow your gut—putrid is bad, but funky is the goal.

FERMENTED CHILE PASTE

Yields about 1 pint

1 lb fresh Fresno chiles
or long peppers,
stemmed and cut into
1 to 2 in pieces

½ oz kosher salt (that's
3 percent of the weight
of the peppers, we did
the math for you!)

To coax out the juices of vegetables with high water content, massage them with salt. This is how it's done with classic sauerkraut. Try it out on peppers (any variety will do) with this chile paste recipe, or fermented shiso for our Shiso Martini (page 64), and then experiment with other water-laden vegetables like cabbage, cucumbers, and peppers. It's advisable to wear kitchen gloves when you work with fresh hot peppers, or you'll end up rubbing your eyes and cryin'. And please note that the final product will be quite salty, so remember this when adding to sauces and dishes.

With a food processor, mortar and pestle, or a knife, chop or mash the chiles into a rough paste. Add the salt and massage it thoroughly into the chiles. Put the paste in a jar, loosely cover it, and allow it to sit at room temperature, checking periodically for mold growth, for 5 to 10 days. The length of time the paste sits will depend on the temperature in your home, which is impacted by the time of year, ventilation, sunlight, etc. Store in an airtight jar in the refrigerator for up to 6 months.

FERMENTED CHILE BUTTER

Yields 1¼ lbs

1 lb unsalted butter, at
room temperature

½ cup Fermented
Chile Paste
(recipe above)

This unctuous, spicy spread is good on everything. We won't go into too much detail about it here, but it's simple and delicious. Just make it—you won't be sorry.

In a medium bowl, gently whip the room temperature butter with a spoon to spread it out in the bowl. Fold in the fermented chile paste until evenly distributed in the butter. Taste it. Yum. Use on toast, to baste fish or meat, or to bring a soup to a silky finish. Store in the refrigerator for up to 1 month in an airtight container or wrapped in plastic.

PICKLED MUSTARD SEEDS

**Yields about
3 cups**

½ cup yellow mustard seeds

2 Tbsp honey

2 tsp kosher salt

½ tsp Aleppo pepper

½ tsp ground turmeric

2 cups white wine vinegar,
plus more to splash
in at the end

Pickled mustard seeds are a bright pop to have around. Use them to finish any dish, from grilled fish to salads and shrimp cocktail.

In a small saucepan, bring the mustard seeds, honey, salt, Aleppo pepper, turmeric, and vinegar to a gentle simmer over medium heat. Continue simmering until the mustard seeds plump up and absorb most of the liquid, about 10 minutes. The pickled mustard seeds should be viscous but not too thick. If the mixture needs to loosen a bit, add a splash more vinegar. Store in an airtight container for up to 1 year.

Techniques

Deep Frying

Commercial fryers hold a consistent temperature and offer a quick and easy way to make crisp, golden, and delicious food. When we opened Lil' Deb's Oasis, we were on an insanely tight budget and bought our first fryer secondhand. It was such a mad dash to open that we didn't get a chance to test it before our maiden service. You can imagine where this story is going: With a restaurant full of eager customers, we quickly realized that our new/old fryer couldn't hold temperature. After a moment of panic, Carla remembered that her grandmother had serendipitously gifted us her copper paila, a huge cauldron perfect for frying, which she had just brought back from Ecuador. We quickly filled it with oil and stuck in a candy thermometer, monitoring and adjusting the heat as we went. We used the paila for more than a year, until we had saved enough money to buy a brand-new deep fryer. This is all to say, don't be afraid. We know deep frying can be intimidating to the uninitiated, but we believe in you!

RULES OF THUMB:

1. Consider depth, width, and weight when selecting a fry pot. Most of our deep-frying recipes require a minimum of 8 cups of oil, so make sure your vessel can accommodate double or triple that amount, because the oil level will rise as you add whatever it is you're frying. And think about the width, so that when, for example, you fry a whole fish, which will be at least 9 inches long, it will fit in your pot. Weight is equally important. Is your vessel thick and heavy enough to withstand 350°F heat for a sustained period? Cast-iron pots are a great option, as are enameled Dutch ovens, because both will help you maintain consistent heat. Woks are great options too, but they lend themselves better to shallow-fry methods.

2. Keep a deep-fry or candy thermometer on hand. Typically, they come with a handy clip that slips onto the rim of your pot for regular temperature checks, which will be imperative to your ability to control heat as it fluctuates throughout the frying process. If you are without a thermometer, drop a bit of batter into the pot when the oil begins to glisten; the oil is ready when you hear a sizzle and see bubbles rise to the surface.

3. Reserve used fryer oil for a future fry session. Simply allow the oil to cool down completely, and then strain it, discarding any solids, before storing it in an airtight container. Whatever you fry in your oil will imbue it with its flavor, so if you fry a fish in oil, that oil will become fishy. When reusing oil, fry animal proteins and vegetables in separate oils. When the oil becomes dark in color, it's time for it to go. An easy way to dispose of old oil is to pour it (cold) back into its original vessel (save the lid too) and throw it out or, better still, offer it to a company or nonprofit that turns used oil into biodiesel fuel.

4. Safety Note: Hot oil is risky business, so please be mindful and proceed with caution. Do not get any water in your hot oil; if you do, it will splatter and burn you. Keep small children away from the fryer. And do not move the pot of hot oil until it has completely cooled. We love you and want you to be safe, that's all.

FRYING FLOUR

Make a mix of ⅔ rice flour to ⅓ cornstarch. For every cup of flour blend you make, season with 1 tsp kosher salt and 1 tsp Magic Dust (page 35). We recommend making the flour in big batches, so you have it whenever you need it.

Making Stocks

Making a good stock is the first step in preparing most soups and some braises, and stocks are also incredible served on their own. Stocks are typically made from bones, but they can also be infused with wonderful flavor from vegetables, which can form the base of a stock on their own or be added partway through the cooking process for a bone-based stock. Roasting the bones before cooking creates a richer flavor and a darker color; cooking them raw yields a more delicately flavored and lighter colored broth.

Aromatics are the foundation of flavor for any stock. We save scraps all week to add to the stock pot. Since you will likely cook stock less frequently than we do, we suggest that you keep a bag of scraps in the freezer and use as needed. Garlic, onions (white or yellow), scallions, shallots, carrots, celery, ginger, bay leaf, lemongrass, parsley, thyme, leeks, and mushroom caps and stems are all good stock builders. Avoid brassicas like broccoli, cauliflower, and cabbage, as well as red onion and radishes, as they tend to either give stocks a sulfuric quality or turn them gray.

FISH/SEAFOOD STOCK

Ask your fishmonger for fish bones and shellfish shells, which are sometimes offered for free or at a discount. Fish stock cooks for less time than its land-animal counterparts—only about 45 minutes to 1 hour—as delicate fish bones and shells break down faster and take less time to infuse the water.

VEGETABLE STOCK

Use whole veggies or scraps, either roasted or raw. Consider leaving the skins on your onions for a deeper golden color in your final stock. Vegetable stock should simmer for 1 to 1½ hours.

POULTRY

Made from the bones, feet, and gizzards of duck, chicken, or turkey, these stocks should cook for a minimum of 2 hours and up to 4 hours.

PORK AND BEEF

Stocks made from pork and beef bones need to cook for a minimum of 3 hours (and a maximum of 8 hours), as the bones take longer to break down and release their nutrients and flavors than bones from smaller game.

RULES OF THUMB:

1. Start your stock in cold water. This will allow impurities to rise to the surface as the temperature rises.

2. Skim your stock. Foam will form on the surface of your stock as it cooks. Skim and repeat until no more foam collects. This process removes denatured proteins and impurities, creating a more beautiful broth and ensuring better temperature control. When foam is allowed to build up, it traps heat beneath the surface, preventing necessary reduction from occurring.

3. Simmer, don't boil. Stocks need to be coaxed gently out of their shells. When boiled and stirred, stocks become cloudy, rather than clear. Look for some small bubbles rising to the surface; do not bring stock to a rolling boil.

4. Salt at the end, not the beginning. Stocks are a practice in patience and a product of reduction. Reduction intensifies flavor. Salting at the beginning makes the final salt level of the product difficult to control, as the saltiness will continue intensifying as it cooks down. Taste your stock at the end of its cook time and salt from there. Salt should amplify but not overpower the flavors already present in the stock.

CHAPTER TWO
LUBRICATION

LUSCIOUS LIBATIONS TO QUENCH YOUR THIRST

RECIPES

Slip between the sheets of this chapter for recipes that have a little something for everyone. More than a simple companion to accompany a meal, our beverage recipes are an opportunity to use fresh and healthy ingredients to start your morning (Sun Ray Smoothie, page 54), cure your hangover (Umeboshi Suero, page 54), treat your friends, lovers, and frenemies to a lovingly crafted cocktail, or dip into a sensual bottle of vino while writing poetry.

Good Vibrations: From the Inside Out

COCO DREAM

Serves 1

1 cup unsweetened
full-fat coconut milk
2 Tbsp simple syrup
(see headnote)
Ice

This recipe is based on a drink often found in Latin America called "agua de coco." It features lightly sweetened fresh coconut milk, with bits of coconut meat, and it is typically served in twist-tied little plastic baggies and sipped with a straw. Fresh coconuts are hard to come by in our town, so we use all-natural, unsweetened coconut milk and adjust the sweetness by adding simple syrup (a 1:1 ratio of sugar and water, heated until the sugar dissolves). Coco Dream is a frothy and refreshing delight.

In a stainless-steel cocktail shaker, combine the coconut milk, simple syrup, and 2 Tbsp of water.

Fill with ice and shake, forcefully moving the ingredients from top to bottom to crush the ice and froth the milk. When the shaker becomes frosty on the outside and nearly too cold to hold, pour into a glass filled with ice and drink. Enjoy on a hot day.

OAT DRINK

Serves 4

1 cup passion fruit purée
1 cup palm sugar or dark
brown sugar
¼ cup rolled oats
1 cinnamon stick

Tangy and lightly sweetened, this passion fruit–focused beverage is cloaked in the gentle hug of oats. In Ecuador, this drink is traditionally made with naranjilla, known as "the golden fruit of the Andes," but variations are also made with pineapple and a mountain papaya called babaco. For a thinner drink, adjust to your liking with additional water.

In a medium saucepan, combine the passion fruit purée, palm sugar, rolled oats, cinnamon stick, and 4 cups of water. Bring to a simmer over medium heat. Continue simmering, stirring occasionally to prevent the oats from sticking or burning, until the oats are soft and incorporated with the liquid, about 20 minutes. Turn off the heat and allow to cool slightly. In a high-speed blender, blend the passion fruit mixture on high until smooth. Pour through a fine-mesh sieve and discard any unground spices. Enjoy hot or cold!

SPAGUA

Yield depends on your ingredient choices

For citrus fruit, cut into
     rounds; for herbs,
     use leaves and stems
     or sprigs
Cucumbers, striped
     and cut into rounds
Chamomile sprigs
Mint sprigs
Lemon verbena leaves
Lovage sprigs
Apples slices
Melon, sliced into
     long slivers
Dill flowers (or any edible
     flowers, really)
Cilantro sprigs
Jalapeño, cut into rounds
Whole shiso leaves
Berries macerated in sugar
Fennel frond stalks
Ice

OK, this is going to be the first of many open-ended recipes—get ready!!!! It is not a new idea, or something originally ours: spa water, our research shows, has been popular for centuries. But in the rush of modern life, the simple pleasure of herb- and citrus-infused water is easily forgotten, so we are here to remind you of its joyful benefits. We serve pitchers of spagua as a peace offering to guests who are waiting for a table on sweltering summer nights. Because who doesn't delight in a gorgeously arranged and refreshing beverage? This summer drink is best enjoyed with products harvested fresh from your (or someone else's) garden.

Combine your choice of herbs, flowers, and fruit in a pitcher with ice. Pour over sparkling, still, or tap water and let marinate for several minutes before serving. Add more water to the mixture as needed.

SUN RAY SMOOTHIE

Serves 1

½ cup Greek yogurt
½ cup orange juice
¼ cup passion fruit purée
1 ripe banana
1 Tbsp flax seeds
1 in piece of ginger, peeled
  and grated
½ tsp ground turmeric
½ cup ice

Full of fiber, potassium, protein, vitamins C and D, and antioxidants, this hearty, healthy meal-in-a-glass is just what you need to start your day. Your body will thank you.

In a blender, combine the yogurt, orange juice, passion fruit purée, banana, flax seeds, ginger, turmeric, and ice and blend on high until smooth. Now, get out there and take on the day!

UMEBOSHI SUERO

Serves 1

1 oz umeboshi vinegar
Juice of 1 lime
Ice
8 oz mineral water
  or seltzer

In Mexico and other parts of Latin America, home remedies called "sueros" are used to treat dehydration and hangovers. Our spin also works as an antidote to afternoon sluggishness or simply as a salty-sour refreshment du jour. The umeboshi alkalinizes your blood and fights nausea, while the lime juice energizes and improves digestion.

In a tall glass, combine the vinegar, lime juice, and ice, adjusting the quantities to your liking. Top with mineral water and enjoy.

LECHE DE TIGRE

Serves 4

2 cups fresh orange juice
1 cup freshly squeezed
    lime juice (from about
    8 limes)
One 3 in piece fresh
    turmeric
One 2 in piece ginger,
    peeled and thinly sliced
1 jalapeño, seeded and
    chopped
2 garlic cloves, peeled
Kosher salt
Fragrant Chile Oil (page 38)
    and mint sprigs
    for serving

Originating in Peru and popular in other coastal locales in South America, the liquid that is used to marinate ceviche is also sold as a wellness tonic. It is said to improve male virility, cure the common cold, decrease the effects of a hangover, and act as an aphrodisiac. Our version of "tiger's milk" is vegetarian. You can think of it as a wellness shot, and, bonus prize, it tastes really good.

In a blender, combine the orange juice, lime juice, turmeric, ginger, jalapeño, and garlic and blend on high until smooth. Pour through a fine-mesh sieve into a glass measuring cup or pitcher; discard any solids. Season with salt, then divide among glasses, drizzle with chile oil, garnish with mint, and serve.

IMMUNE SHROOM

Serves 4

¼ cup pearled barley
4 tsp chaga mushroom
    powder
1½ Tbsp cocoa powder
¼ tsp freshly ground
    black pepper
About ¼ cup honey

This immunity-boosting bev is a playful baby born from traditional drinks like horchata and barley water. Slightly sweet, nourishing, and surprisingly filling, it is delicious served hot or cold. It also features chaga mushrooms, which are believed to reduce inflammation, balance blood pressure, and protect against cancer.

In a stockpot, combine the barley, chaga mushroom powder, cocoa powder, pepper, and 8 cups of water. Bring to a boil over medium-high heat. Turn the heat to low and simmer until the barley is fully cooked, soft throughout and doubled in size, and the mixture has thickened, about 30 minutes. Turn off the heat and gradually stir in the honey, adding a little bit at a time and tasting until it reaches your desired level of sweetness. Pour through a fine-mesh sieve, reserving 2 Tbsp of the cooked barley and discarding the rest. Serve hot, or allow to cool completely and serve over ice, spooning the reserved barley on top—for a fun little toothsome addition.

Next page: Health and wellness elixirs, from left to right: Umeboshi Suero, Leche de Tigre, Immune Shroom

MATÉ LATTE

Serves 2 to 4

2 cups whole milk or
    half-and-half
6 Tbsp dried maté
1 Tbsp chamomile flowers
    (or one chamomile
    tea bag)
2 tsp ground turmeric
¼ tsp freshly ground
    black pepper
5 cloves
3 cardamom pods,
    smashed
1 cinnamon stick
2 to 3 Tbsp honey

A blasphemy to Argentineans everywhere, we've added a whole bunch of stuff to the already-perfect, deeply grassy flavors of yerba maté. Maté was originally consumed by the Guarani and Tupi peoples of modern day Bolivia, Argentina, Paraguay, and Uruguay and still holds a strong cultural significance to these countries today. It has more antioxidants than green tea, and the addition of milk and spices brings our version straight into chai territory, providing warmth, comfort, and energy. Sorry, we know it's a sin, but guess what? Sinners have more fun.

In a small saucepan, combine the milk, maté, chamomile flowers, turmeric, pepper, cloves, cardamom, cinnamon, and 1 cup of water. Add as much honey as you like, then place over low heat and simmer gently, stirring occasionally to keep a film from forming on the surface, until the spices are infused into the milk, about 20 minutes. Pour through a fine-mesh sieve and discard any solids. Enjoy hot or cold.

THE MORNING-AFTER COFFEE

Serves 2 to 4

One 14 oz can
    unsweetened, full-fat
    coconut milk
One 14 oz can sweetened
    condensed milk
6 Tbsp finely ground coffee
1 in piece of ginger, grated

A cup of this drink gives us enough zing to get through the day's prep list. We aren't trying to reinvent the wheel of your morning ritual, but we do hope to spice up your day a little bit. Perfect to serve to a lover you want to see again. If not using a French press, ginger can be added at the end of the percolation process.

In a medium bowl, whisk together the coconut milk and sweetened condensed milk. Use right away to make coffee or store in an airtight container in the refrigerator for up to 1 week. This coconut and condensed milk concoction will make about a week's worth of coffee.

In a 32 oz French press, combine the coffee and ginger, cover with boiling water, stir, and insert the plunger. Let steep for about 5 minutes then slowly press down the plunger and pour into mugs. Add as much of the coconut and condensed milk concoction as your heart desires. Stir. Enjoy the extra jolt of the ginger root.

Lowered Inhibitions: Cocktails

There is nothing more glamorous than a delicious cocktail. The only thing more glam is having the skills to make one yourself. Dive into our cocktail section and learn how to wow your guests at dinner parties, or how to amaze your own damn self after a long day. Feel what it's like to make a little magic as you learn to make infusions, fermentations, and several staples from our cocktail menu.

GARDEN ORGY

Serves 1

2 to 3 sprigs cilantro, plus
    more for garnish
½ oz simple syrup
    (see page 52)
¾ oz freshly squeezed lime
    juice, plus 1 lime slice
    for garnish
2 to 3 slices of jalapeño
2 oz good quality tequila
Ice

As a carpenter and sculptor, our first bar manager, Sean Desiree, has instinct and skill in creating balance that is felt in this cocktail, which made its debut on our very first menu. Citrus, herbs, sweetness, and spice are all represented in a drink that has no starring roles but is instead a perfect ensemble. (Isn't that what a good orgy is all about?) When it comes to tequila, we prefer La Gritona, because it's woman-owned and operated and comes in recycled glass bottles. Here, we muddle the jalapeño to order, but you can also infuse an entire 750 ml bottle of tequila with jalapeño. Cut half a jalapeño into slices, add to the tequila, and let infuse for at least 1 day. This will make a very different drink, as you'll get to experience the subtle flavor produced through the leaching of oils from the chile skins into the tequila over time.

In a stainless-steel cocktail shaker, add the cilantro and simple syrup. Don't be shy with the cilantro and do not remove the stems, as they hold a lot of good juice. With an unvarnished wooden spoon or cocktail muddler, press down lightly on the leaves and give them a few gentle twists (pressing too hard releases the herb's bitter chlorophyll). Once the aroma of cilantro has been released, add the lime juice, jalapeño, and tequila.

Fill the shaker three-quarters full with ice and shake until the outside of the shaker is super frosty, about 10 seconds. Strain into a coupe glass if you're fancy! The drink should have very small, floating pieces of cilantro, a lot of chipped ice, and a light green hue. Garnish with a sprig of cilantro and a slice of lime.

Opposite: Jaime, a former bar manager, is a fabulous Leo who loves Dolly Parton, bunnies, long walks on the beach, and universal healthcare. They are the coauthor of these cocktail recipes.

MAGIC MOUNTAIN

Serves 1

Burnt Honey Syrup

½ cup honey

Magic Mountain

¾ oz lemon juice, plus a
    lemon peel for garnish

3 slices fresh turmeric

2 oz mezcal

¾ oz burnt honey syrup

1 sage leaf, for garnish

Working from a Scotch cocktail called The Witch, we substituted the peat moss smoke of Scotch for the wood smoke of mezcal, with the option to add aroma from sage smoke. Though it's elemental to culinary culture, the flavor we call smoke is mostly a reaction to smell and memory. Korean American chef Edward Lee, author of *Smoke and Pickles: Recipes and Stories from a New Southern Kitchen*, calls it the sixth taste after sweet, sour, salty, bitter, and umami. The combined elements of "smoke" in this cocktail—the wood smoke of the mezcal, the burnt smoke of the honey, and the herbal smoke of the holy sage—create a potent portal for the restoration of memory.

TO MAKE THE BURNT HONEY SYRUP: In a small pan, stir the honey over medium heat until it starts to bubble, turns a dark golden brown, and gives off a slight burnt caramel smell. Immediately remove from the heat and add 2 tsp of water, stirring quickly and carefully to fully dissolve. Use right away to make cocktails or store in an airtight container in the refrigerator for up to 3 months.

TO MAKE THE MAGIC MOUNTAIN: In a stainless-steel cocktail shaker, combine the lemon juice and turmeric. With an unvarnished wooden spoon or cocktail muddler, pound on the turmeric to muddle it. Add the mezcal and burnt honey syrup. Fill the shaker half full with ice and shake until the outside of the shaker begins to frost. Strain the drink into a rocks glass over ice, using a large format cube if you have one. Garnish with lemon peel, first expressing the oils from the peel by gently squeezing it over the cocktail, then rolling into the shape of a rosebud and placing it gently on the surface of the ice. Set the drink before your guest, light the sage leaf on fire, and place it on top of the peel.

Wanna drink an evergreen campfire? Take this drink a step further by infusing it with sage smoke—to bring out campfire memories—right before serving. Before shaking the cocktail mixture, place a sage bundle or several sage leaves on a small plate, and set aflame. When the smoke begins to billow, quickly cover it with your serving glass, where the smoke will begin to collect. Quickly shake the drink and strain it into the smoke-filled glass.

SHISO MARTINI

Serves 1

Shiso Brine
2 bunches purple shiso
Kosher salt
Non-chlorinated filtered
   water

Shiso Martini
3 oz good-quality gin,
   preferably from a local
   small-batch distiller
½ oz Dolin Dry Vermouth
¼ oz freshly squeezed
   lime juice
½ oz shiso brine
½ oz umeboshi vinegar
Ice
Shiso leaf, for garnish

After a summer of fermenting shiso for other purposes, it occurred to us that the magenta juices released when the leaves ferment would make an incredible substitute for the olive brine typically used to make a dirty martini. From the mint family and native to the mountains of China and India, red shiso, or akajiso, is often used as a fresh herb on sushi or sashimi platters or as an important component in making umeboshi; it can also be dried and added to furikake. Its mountain meadow taste is bright and vibrant, like a mélange of mint, basil, tarragon, and anise. You'll need to begin the shiso fermentation process several days before you serve this drink—trust us, it's worth the wait!

TO MAKE THE SHISO BRINE: Separate the shiso leaves from the stems. Using a sharp knife, cut, chiffonade style, into thin slivers. Weigh the leaves in grams and take note of their weight. Use enough kosher salt to equal 3 percent of the weight of the leaves. For example, if the leaves weigh 20 grams, use .6 gram of salt. In a bowl, sprinkle the salt over the leaves and massage them with your hands. Let stand for at least 2 hours at room temperature, so the leaves can release their juices. Pack the leaves and their juices into an appropriately sized jar and add enough filtered water to cover. To ferment, loosely close the lid to allow some air to enter and keep the jar at room temperature for 3 to 7 days. The brine should be a deep purple and taste herbal, peppery, salty, and slightly acidic. It can be refrigerated in an airtight container for up to 1 year.

TO MAKE THE SHISO MARTINI: In a stainless-steel cocktail shaker, combine the gin, vermouth, lime juice, shiso brine, and vinegar. Fill the shaker with ice and shake until the outside of the shaker is frosty. Strain the drink into a martini glass and garnish with a shiso leaf. Sip slowly and enjoy.

From left to right: Giallo Moon, Shiso Martini, Tutti Frutti Trashy Cutie, Garden Orgy, Dirty Fingers

DIRTY FINGERS

Serves 1

2 oz fresh carrot juice
1 oz freshly squeezed
    lemon juice
¼ oz fresh ginger juice
1½ oz mezcal
1½ oz Italian-style herbal
    liqueur, such as
    Forthave Red or
    Campari

Seasonal, healthy, local ingredients have always been part of our practice at Lil' Deb's Oasis, but they became a self-imposed constraint for our COVID-19 pandemic picnic project, Fuego 69. Carrots are a great cold and cough remedy, especially when paired with lemon. Ginger is a powerful antioxidant and anti-inflammatory for the lungs. Some say mezcal is the healthiest spirit, as it's mostly produced in very small batches on family-owned farms, and it rarely contains additives, like sugar or chemicals, commonly used in the production of other alcohols. Add the handmade, ruby-hued aperitivo Forthave Red, which is produced in Brooklyn with a bounty of botanical herbs, and you've got a delicious healthy-ish bev that packs a punch. If juicing your carrots and ginger is not an option, you can purchase bottled versions of the juice ingredients, except the lemon, which, we beg you, only use fresh!

In a glass, stir together the carrot juice, lemon juice, ginger juice, mezcal, and liqueur. Serve over ice.

TUTTI FRUTTI TRASHY CUTIE (T.F.T.C.)

Serves 1

1½ oz fresh pineapple juice
1½ oz compost-infused
    vodka (1-week
    minimum infusion)
1 oz white vermouth,
    such as Dolin Blanc
    Vermouth de Chambéry
Ice
Paper umbrella, pineapple
    leaf or slice, or edible
    flower, for garnish

Sustainability isn't just about recycling programs. It's about perceptions and value judgments and what is considered worthwhile or worthless. There's nothing more Lil' Deb's Oasis than body-centered awareness of worth and everything that ripples out from it. It's with those eyes that we look at our bar scraps of bright citrus, fruit, and herbs, and think, "Let's give you a second act, gorgeous!" Rather than throwing it away, we are inspired by this "waste material." It's a lot of fun using vegetable, herb, citrus, and even tea scraps that otherwise would have gone in the compost bin to create boozy ambrosial infusions that are so delicious you could drink them neat or over ice. Our original recipe includes leftover hibiscus flowers (steeped for our house-made tea), the rinds of lemons and limes, fennel scraps, jalapeño stems and ribs, and herb stems. Be creative with yours!

COMPOST-INFUSED BOOZE "RECIPE": Buy a bottle of decent booze. Vodka and tequila work well because of their generally neutral flavors. Save food scraps from every meal you eat for a week. Citrus rinds, verdant veggie scraps (not brassicas like kale, cabbage, etc.), and herb stems are all good choices, but try to look at your food scraps a little differently. Experiment with leftover tea bags, fruit pits, fruit skins and just make it fun! In a jar with an airtight seal, pour your alcohol of choice over the scraps you've saved, making sure all the ingredients are well submerged. Seal and refrigerate for 3 days to 1 week. Strain and discard any solids. Store in an airtight container in the refrigerator—alcohol-based infusions will last for a year in the fridge.

RULES OF INFUSION:
❋ The amount of ingredients and infusion time will determine taste and aroma: The longer you infuse and the more ingredients you use, the stronger the flavors will be.
❋ With citrus that's already been juiced, infuse for at least a week to allow all the oils to leech out of the citrus rind and impart their flavor.
❋ Some ingredients, such as beets, hibiscus, and turmeric, will also leech color and give you some sexy *lewks*.
❋ Chile peppers and other spicy ingredients should be removed after a day to limit the heat, depending on your preferred spice levels.
❋ Taste the infusion every day—to help keep the doctor away. If you choose to remove the peppers before a week is up, allow your other ingredients to keep on vibing.

HERE'S A RECIPE TO MAKE A FANCY VERSION OF THIS COCKTAIL: In a stainless-steel cocktail shaker, combine the pineapple juice, vodka, and vermouth. Add about 5 ice cubes and shake until the outside of the shaker is cold to the touch. Strain into a rocks glass, add ice, and garnish with a paper umbrella, a pineapple leaf or slice, or an edible flower.

GIALLO MOON

Serves 1

Saffron-Infused Gin

Small pinch of saffron

One 750 ml bottle good-
quality small-batch gin

Rooibos Ice

3 rooibos tea bags

Giallo Moon

1 oz freshly squeezed
lemon juice, plus a
lemon twist for garnish

1 oz saffron-infused gin

½ oz Strega

½ oz Meletti

4 dashes Angostura bitters

This cauldron of botanical maximalism is our unauthorized fan fiction for the Italian herbal liqueurs called amari. These bitter liqueurs are centuries old and were developed as curatives to heal a variety of ailments. Often made with more than seventy different herbs and aromatics, amari are as varied as the regional botanicals they are crafted from, with recipes that are prized and protected family secrets. Bright yellow Strega, which is used here, is said to be a love elixir given to the Alberti family as an expression of gratitude, after a young son rescued a witch ("strega" in Italian) from falling out of a tree. Amari are meant to be sipped slowly after a meal to aid digestion, and we certainly recommend doing so, but below we celebrate some of our favorites by combining two of these inscrutable beauties in a single cocktail.

We suggest choosing one of the "new wave" gins, which tend to be less bitter and less juniper-focused than a classic dry gin. Our absolute favorite is the unfiltered Forthave Blue, which pairs well with the strong botanicals of the liqueurs, due to its own complex botanical makeup. Don't forget to infuse your gin and make your ice cubes ahead of time! You can use a regular ice cube tray to make the cubes, but we also love the silicone ice trays that come in different shapes and sizes and recommend investing in at least one tray of larger than normal ice cubes, as they have a lower melting point than regular cubes.

TO MAKE THE SAFFRON-INFUSED GIN: Add a small pinch of saffron—a little goes a long way—to the bottle of gin. Let it sit for a day or more, or until it turns a bright orange color. Use right away to make cocktails or store indefinitely.

TO MAKE THE ROOIBOS ICE: Steep the rooibos tea in 2 cups of hot water for 10 minutes. Remove and discard the tea bags. Pour the tea into an ice cube tray and freeze until solid.

TO MAKE THE GIALLO MOON: In a stainless-steel cocktail shaker, combine the lemon juice, gin, Strega, Meletti, and bitters. Fill the shaker half full with ice and shake for ten seconds. Strain into a low-ball glass and garnish with a lemon twist.

Wine Journeys

Building a wine vocabulary is a lot like learning how to talk about art. The language seems so beautiful, yet it's institutional, intimidating, and full of insider jargon. We haven't been formally trained as sommeliers, so when we began to order wine for the restaurant, we became wine sponges, soaking up every drop of knowledge that books, wine reps, and local bottle shops had to offer. We already knew we wanted to serve exclusively natural wine, but we knew we'd have to convince some of our customers to give it a try.

We instructed our servers to ask diners what wines they enjoyed, so that they could recommend a natural wine with similar qualities. But we were trying to fit the wines we had chosen into conventional boxes when we had chosen them *because* they didn't fit into conventional boxes. A sediment-heavy, amber-colored Chardonnay from Slovenia will never satisfy someone who wants a traditional oaky, buttery Chardonnay, and the tasting process with the customer will always lead to disappointment because the natural wine won't satisfy their conventional craving.

By wanting to learn about natural wine, we had unknowingly begun to seek the approval of the institution of wine. We came to realize that just because natural winemakers reject some of the practices of capitalism and imperialism, an industry predominantly run by cis white people will inevitably have institutional qualities, no matter how honorable its sustainable agricultural practices. Our reaction to this epiphany was to recommit to making information accessible and to reject taste hierarchies.

The energy in our restaurant acts as a litmus test of sorts: The room is pink and warm and loud and queer, so when people walk through our doors, they tend to come with an open mind. In fact, they often come to us because they *want* their tastes to be expanded. We aim for our wine list to invite adventure through inclusion and provide comfort through wine poems (page 169). We also re-envisioned our wine service to be more connective and fun through what we call wine journeys, a choose-your-own-adventure approach to wine selection. By diving into the absurd and abstract, we attempt to break down the rules that can be limiting or intimidating to those not versed in wine language.

A wine journey is best embarked upon when hosting a dinner party, but it can also be a solo experience when you find yourself staring at a wall of unfamiliar labels at the wine shop.

What Is a Wine Journey?

CUSTOMER: "I want a red wine."

SERVER: "If you had a cabin in the woods, would you rather have a wood stove and a bear skin rug inside, or a jacuzzi outside?"

This was our first wine journey, born from a heat of the moment, mid-service pivot. Wine journeys evolved from our desire to help customers select a wine without basing our questions in the conventional, and often exclusionary, framework of wine language. Much like you need to develop your own relationship to your palate when seasoning food, when guiding a wine journey, it's essential to find your own sense of direction.

When beginning your wine journey as a dinner party host, start with a small selection of wines—say, three bottles—that you are familiar with and love. It's important to pose open-ended questions that invite specific, sensual, and creative answers. We always start with questions related to texture, temperature, color, place, and sensual experiences in general, because the answers you get will help distinguish among the bottles you have to work with. For example, if you have a heavy red, a sparkling orange, and a sleek white, but all three wines are bone dry, you want to think in terms of texture and character rather than dryness.

Take a Journey:

QUESTION: If you could go swimming right now in any place, in any kind of water, what would you choose? Specify the temperature of the water and the air.

ANSWER A: A swimming hole, at sunrise, when the water is cold but refreshing.

LOGIC: If someone says swimming hole, they're OK with getting a little freaky. If this person had said "pool," they may be craving something more straightforward. The combination of the morning light and the temperature of the water leads us to believe they crave lightness. If the person had said "sunset," the wine could have been either an orange or a light gemstone-colored red wine.

WINE: Go for a cloudy rosé that's tart but not overly acidic.

THEY DON'T LIKE IT, SO TRY ANOTHER WINE: A dry, yet pillowy soft rosé.

ANSWER B: Saltwater pool, nighttime, the moon is full, and the water is the same temp as the air; no clothes are worn.

LOGIC: This person wants pure luxury and perfect sensations. What matters most about this experience is that it feels effortlessness, while still being luxurious, as evidenced by the saltwater pool, the temperature, the night air, and the nudity.

WINE: The textures evoked by this answer lead us to a velvety red from a region that can produce a savory, softer-spoken wine, most likely in France.

THEY DON'T LIKE IT, SO TRY ANOTHER WINE: a gorgeous, amber-colored orange wine, most likely Italian. We might not know why the person doesn't want red; we just know it's time to pivot. An amber orange wine has the same grown-up feeling as a light red wine; it's a little more serious in terms of its tannin level but more playful in terms of its acid level, which balances the scales and makes it a good alternative to red.

CHAPTER THREE
FOREPLAY

SEXY FOODS TO DELIGHT THE TASTE BUDS AND PIQUE THE SENSUAL INTERESTS

RECIPES

The recipes in this chapter are designed to whet the palate and make you hungry for more. Whether for a sprawling drinks party or an intimate soiree, this is the kind of eating we love: time passes barely noticed as sumptuous little bites of sassy, playful food are consumed. You'll find that the right set of snacks can deliciously prolong a gathering by satisfying your hungry guests right from the start and letting them slowly wind their way through the evening before you're ready to reveal the main course. Of course, some of the best party menus consist exclusively of appetizers for guests to graze on, because who wants to hold a big plate of food while flirting with a new friend in a crowded kitchen? One thing leads to another and the next thing you know you're unbuttoning your pants—not because you're too full but because you want to make room for more. Weave your way through this chapter and open your mind and belly because there's more to come…

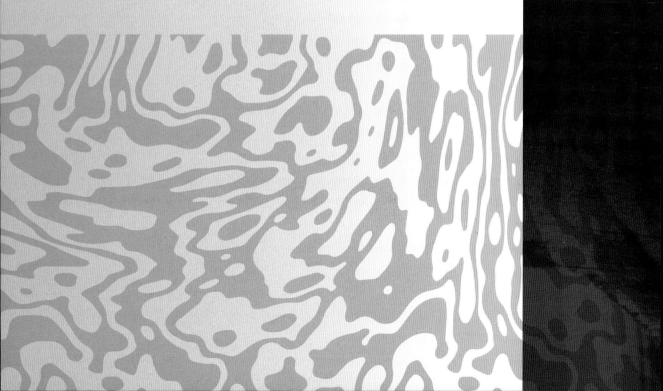

WISH YOU WERE HERE!
XOXO,
MIAMI

SWEET PLANTAINS WITH GREEN CREAM

Serves 4 to 6

Green Cream

One 17.6 oz container
    Greek yogurt or labneh
4 cups coarsely chopped
    and loosely packed
    cilantro leaves and
    stems
1 cup extra-virgin olive oil
½ cup freshly squeezed
    lime juice (from about
    4 limes)
1 Tbsp kosher salt

Plantains

4 cups canola oil
4 to 6 super ripe plantains
Kosher salt

We can hardly find words to introduce this simple classic that has been on our menu since day one. A frequent question from our customers is: "Just WHAT is in the sauce!?" And now, you know the answer too. We think it produces better results, but if deep frying isn't your bag, a shallow fry will do—simply heat a few tablespoons of oil in a pan to fry your plantains.

TO MAKE THE GREEN CREAM: Put the yogurt in a medium bowl and set aside.

In a blender, combine the cilantro, olive oil, lime juice, and salt and blend until fully incorporated and smooth—you may need to let your blender rest, so it doesn't overheat, or the cilantro may turn brown. Add to the yogurt and whisk briskly until fully incorporated. Season with additional salt, if desired. Cover and refrigerate until ready to serve.

TO MAKE THE PLANTAINS: In a medium-size heavy-bottomed pot over medium-high or a deep fryer, heat the canola oil to 350°F on a deep-fry thermometer (see frying guidelines, page 45). Line a baking sheet with a paper bag and set near the stove or deep fryer.

Peel the plantains and cut them on a bias, so the pieces are long and angular.

When the oil reaches 350°F, carefully add 6 to 8 plantain pieces and fry, turning with tongs or a slotted spoon, until the plantains are a deep, rich color that just kisses the edge of burnt, about 2 minutes per side. The sugars in the plantains begin to truly caramelize at this stage, leaving you with a crispy outside and an irresistibly gooey inside. Transfer the plantains to the paper bag–lined baking sheet and season with salt. Fry the remaining plantains, adjusting the heat as needed to keep the oil at 350°F.

TO SERVE: Use a large spoon to schmear green cream on the bottom of a plate, artfully arranging the fried plantains on top; alternatively, serve the sauce on the side and dip liberally.

Pro Tip

When shopping, look for soft, black- and yellow-mottled plantains. If you can't find super ripe plantains, before peeling and cutting them, hold a yellow plantain in both hands and firmly apply pressure, squeezing your hands across its length with confidence, but without crushing it. (Yes, exactly like you're performing a delightfully firm erotic massage. We told you food was sexy!) Continue massaging until the plantain begins to soften slightly. The goal is to maintain the integrity of the plantain while softening its form.

YUCA WITH HERB CHIMICHURRI

Serves 4 to 6

Chimichurri

1 bunch scallions
½ cup canola oil
1 bunch flat-leaf parsley
¼ cup extra-virgin olive oil
Juice and zest of 3 limes
10 garlic cloves, minced
2 Tbsp dried oregano
1 Tbsp kosher salt
(or to taste!)

Yuca

4 to 5 lbs yuca, each
about 3 in in diameter
4 cups canola oil
(only if frying)
2 cups heavy cream
(only if mashing)
1 stick unsalted butter,
at room temperature
(only if mashing)
Kosher salt

Shopping tip

Always add an extra pound
of yuca to your shopping list,
or check the yuca's quality while
you shop by cracking it in half.
Yuca flesh should be bright
white and smell starchy fresh.
Discard pieces with black- or
brown-spotted flesh or a slightly
funky, fermented odor.

Yuca, the artist also known as cassava, is an immensely versatile root, and, like a potato, it can be used in soups, stews, and braises, as well as fried solo or mashed. Its starch, commonly known as tapioca starch, makes a wonderful option for gluten-free flour, and can be used to make doughs and breads.

We give you two options for this dish: crispy fries and a decadent mash. Both are divine. But before you start, a warning about yuca: It must be cooked thoroughly, as it contains high levels of cyanide that must be cooked out to eliminate the risk of cyanide poisoning. Don't stress about it though—just follow our recipe, which fully cooks the yuca, and know that the only risk you're taking is that you might keel over from total pleasure overload. And who doesn't love living a little dangerously?

TO MAKE THE CHIMICHURRI: In a medium pot, bring 8 cups of generously salted water (it should taste like the ocean) to a boil. In a medium bowl, make an ice bath of half ice and half water. Submerge the scallions in the boiling water and blanch for 10 seconds. Immediately plunge into the ice bath to stop the cooking process, then drain, squeeze out any water, and pat dry. Put the scallions in a blender, add the canola oil, and blend until smooth. Transfer to a medium bowl and set aside.

Using a sharp knife and smooth tight cuts to avoid bruising, cut the parsley stems and leaves, chiffonade style, into thin slivers. Add to the scallion mixture, along with the olive oil, lime zest and juice, garlic, oregano, and salt. Whisk to combine and set aside.

TO MAKE THE YUCA: Bring a large pot of generously salted water to a boil.

Meanwhile, using a large kitchen knife, remove the ends of the yuca and bisect each piece into two flat halves. Place one hand firmly on top of the yuca. Use the knife to peel off the waxy brown skin, moving the piece of yuca in a slightly circular motion as you work your way around. Once peeled, cut each yuca half into quarters that are roughly 1 in wide and 4 in long. They will be mashed or fried to a crisp, so perfection is not essential :)

Once the water comes to a boil, gently add the yuca and cook for at least 15 minutes. Yuca is fully cooked when it is soft, with no hard center, and slightly translucent. Depending on how fresh the yuca is, this may take up to 25 minutes. Using a mesh strainer or a slotted spoon, remove the yuca from the pot and drain the water. If frying, place the yuca on a wire rack until cool to the touch. If mashing, remove and discard the thick vein from the center of each piece of yuca, then return it to the empty pot.

TO FRY THE YUCA: In a medium heavy-bottomed pot over medium-high or in a deep fryer, heat the canola oil to 350°F on a deep-fry thermometer (see frying guidelines, page 45). Line a baking sheet with a paper bag or paper towels and set near the stove or deep fryer.

When the oil reaches 350°F, carefully add 6 to 8 pieces of yuca and fry, turning with tongs or a slotted spoon, until golden brown, about 3 minutes. Transfer the yuca to the paper towel–lined baking sheet. Fry the remaining yuca, adjusting the heat as needed to keep the oil at 350°F. Serve immediately with the garlicky chimichurri dipping sauce—don't be shy about your inevitable garlic breath. Just kiss your friends anyway ;)

TO MASH THE YUCA: Using a potato masher or wooden spoon, thoroughly mash the yuca. Put the pot over low heat, then add the heavy cream and butter and stir to fully incorporate. Season with salt as needed. Drizzle generously with chimichurri for serving.

CRUDITES WITH ROMESCO VERDE

Makes 1 party platter

Romesco Verde

3 green bell peppers
1 cup chopped flat-leaf
   parsley
1 cup roasted pistachios
¼ cup white wine vinegar
Zest and juice of 1 lemon
4 garlic cloves
1 fresh serrano chile
   pepper
2 Tbsp salt
1 cup extra-virgin olive oil

Crudités

Classic Catalonian romesco sauce calls for a paste made with lots of nuts, such as almonds or hazelnuts, roasted tomatoes, and dried ñora peppers. We use pistachios, green bell peppers, and parsley to give it garden goddess qualities and pair it with an assortment of the best and brightest vegetables of the season. Some of our favorites include cucumber, fennel, radish or daikon, scallion, carrot, jícama, sweet pepper, cherry tomato, celery, snap pea or any seasonal vine bean, cauliflower, or broccoli. A single vegetable, say carrots, would work, too.

TO MAKE THE ROMESCO VERDE: Under a broiler or on a grill, blacken the green bell peppers, using tongs to rotate the peppers for an even char. Once the skin has blackened but not burned, put the peppers in a bowl, cover with plastic wrap, and steam for at least 10 minutes.

When the peppers have cooled, gently rub your fingers along the charred skin to remove it. Cut the peppers into slivers, discarding the ribs and seeds. Transfer to a blender or food processor then add the parsley, pistachios, vinegar, lemon zest and juice, garlic, serrano pepper, and salt and blend until a rough paste has formed. With the blender or processor running, gradually add the olive oil and continue blending to fully incorporate. Refrigerate until ready to serve or store in an airtight container in the refrigerator for up to a week.

OK, so the next step is crucial and we encourage you to find joy in the process of preparing crudités for presentation. At the restaurant, we argue over who gets to clean the vegetables because the process is so meditative and relaxing. All you need is cool water in the sink or in a bowl, dishcloth or paper towels, a peeler, and a paring knife. Then consider each vegetable's form and how best to clean and cut them to produce a dynamic variety of shapes and sizes. We have some suggestions to make these beautiful vegetables even more beautiful:

* radishes: keep them whole; remove their outer leaves, but leave their inner dainty leaves intact
* peel carrots and then cut them on the bias
* rinse fennel and remove its tough outer layer, before cutting it vertically to reveal its gorgeous, angel-like wings
* peel strips of cucumber skin lengthwise to create alternating rows and then cut into batons
* remove the outer layers of scallions, revealing their bright white skin, and trim their tops at a slight angle to accentuate their zesty personalities
* peel jícama and cut into rods or rounds
* serve peas and runner beans raw or blanched in salted, boiling water for 30 seconds and then shocked in an ice bath for 1 minute to bring out their deeper green hues
* for extra crunch, prepare cauliflower or broccoli raw or blanched

TO SERVE: Select a large, flat-ish platter and schmear a generous amount of romesco down the middle, on a curved line. Arrange vegetables, creating zones of color—this is an art form after all! To distribute color and form throughout the platter, don't be afraid to place veggies in different areas on the board more than once.

MARINATED MUSHROOMS

Serves 2 to 4

Mushrooms

1 lb shiitake or other
  mushrooms
  of your choice
1 cup plus 2 Tbsp canola
  or other neutral oil
1 tsp kosher salt

Marinade

½ cup apple cider vinegar
2 Tbsp kosher salt
1 Tbsp granulated sugar
1 tsp pink, green, or black
  peppercorns
1 tsp allspice berries
4 garlic cloves, smashed
  and peeled
3 bay leaves
1 large carrot, peeled and
  cut into ¼ in rounds
2 bunches scallions

This dish combines many of our favorite textures: As they sit in the green scallion oil, the mushrooms become silky and slippery on your tongue, while the carrots add crunch and color. Enjoy your mushrooms solo, or with toast or eggs, or in a salad. Oh, the many options for this tangy, sweet, deeply savory snack. Plus, the mushrooms hold up so well in the fridge you can make these in bulk and eat them for a whole month!

Place two baking sheets in the oven and preheat the oven to 500°F.

TO PREPARE THE MUSHROOMS: Remove and save the woody stems from the mushrooms (they are great for stocks) then cut large mushrooms to match the size of the smaller ones. In a large bowl, toss the mushrooms with 2 Tbsp of the oil and the salt. Carefully remove the preheated pans from the oven, divide the mushrooms between the pans, and spread out to ensure even browning. Roast until golden caramel brown, 10 to 15 minutes. Put the mushrooms in a bowl and set aside.

TO MAKE THE MARINADE: In a small pot, bring the vinegar, salt, sugar, peppercorns, allspice, garlic, bay leaves, carrot, and ¾ cup of water to a boil, stirring to dissolve the sugar and salt and infuse the spices. Remove from the heat, pour over the mushrooms, and gently toss to coat the mushrooms. Cut 3 of the scallions into 1 in pieces, add to the mushrooms, and toss to combine. Let cool to room temperature.

Bring a small pot of water to a roaring boil. In a medium bowl, make an ice bath of half ice and half water. Submerge the remaining whole scallions in the boiling water and blanch until the brightness of the green becomes more pronounced, about 1 minute. Immediately plunge into the ice bath to stop the cooking process then drain, squeeze out any water, and pat dry. Coarsely chop the scallions then transfer to a blender, add the remaining 1 cup of canola oil, and blend until smooth—try to work quickly so the oil doesn't heat up and discolor the scallions. Add to the mushrooms and toss to combine. Transfer to an airtight container and marinate in the refrigerator overnight or store for up to 2 weeks. Serve at room temperature.

BLISTERED PEPPERS WITH MOLE POWDER

Serves 4

1 Tbsp canola oil
1 lb sweet summer
    peppers, such as
    shishito, Padron,
    Habanada, or lunchbox
3 Tbsp Mole Powder
    (page 36)
Coarse salt

This dish combines two simple things: our mole powder and peppers at the height of their season. Some dishes don't need much explanation, and this is one of them.

In a large cast-iron skillet over high heat, warm the canola oil until smoking hot. Toss the peppers into the skillet and cook, turning with tongs, until they begin to pop and blister, 1 to 2 minutes. Transfer to a serving bowl, add the mole powder, season with coarse salt, and toss to combine. Eat with your fingers!

ELOTE WITH CHARRED COCONUT CREMA

Serves 6

Peanut-Sesame Crumble

¼ cup black sesame seeds

¼ cup white sesame seeds

¼ cup unsweetened desiccated coconut

½ cup roasted, salted peanuts, finely chopped

2 Tbsp sugar

1 tsp salt

Coco Cream

1 cup canola oil

1 shallot, thinly sliced

One 12 oz can unsweetened full-fat coconut milk

1 cup loosely packed cilantro leaves and stems

1 cup roasted, salted peanuts

3 Tbsp fish sauce

Zest and juice of 2 limes

2 garlic cloves

1 serrano pepper, seeded

Corn

6 ears corn, husked and peeled and stem on

Herbs, such as dill, mint, or cilantro, for garnish

Limes, quartered, for serving

This is one of our oldest recipes, created before Lil' Deb's Oasis existed, when Hannah and Carla worked together on a food truck. A play on classic Mexican elote, we substitute the cheese and mayonnaise for charred coconut cream, which we fondly call "coco cream." If making a vegan version, substitute fish sauce with kosher salt, and salt to taste. When done you should have a bitter-sweet, spicy, creamy, nutty sauce that has some body due to the peanuts. The oil used to blacken the shallots can be drained and stored in an airtight container in your refrigerator up to two weeks for the next time you char something.

The ideal way to grill your corn on a hot summer's afternoon is over charcoal—we all know the flavor is better—but propane will work, too. If there's no grill in sight, you can char your corn stovetop style on a hot cast-iron skillet (open a window if need be).

TO MAKE THE PEANUT-SESAME CRUMBLE: In a medium frying pan over medium-low heat, toast the black and white sesame seeds until the white sesame seeds turn fragrant and golden brown, 3 to 5 minutes. Transfer the seeds to a small bowl and return the pan to medium-low heat. Add the coconut and toast until fragrant and golden, 1 to 2 minutes. Add to the bowl of sesame seeds. Add the peanuts and toss to combine. Add the sugar and salt and toss to fully incorporate. Store in an airtight container at room temperature for up to 1 month.

TO MAKE THE COCO CREAM: Line a plate with paper towels and set near the stove. In a medium frying pan over medium-high heat, warm the canola oil. Add the shallot slices and fry beyond what is considered a normal golden brown—take them to black and crispy for a smoky char flavor—about 10 minutes. Transfer to the paper towel–lined plate to drain then put in a blender, add the coconut milk, cilantro, peanuts, fish sauce, lime zest and juice, garlic, and serrano pepper and blend on high until smooth. Refrigerate until the sauce thickens and chill the sauce before serving it with the hot corn.

TO MAKE THE CORN: Heat a gas or charcoal grill to medium-high. Put the corn directly on the grates and grill, turning until charred all over, 5 to 8 minutes. Allow to cool to the touch.

TO SERVE: Using a pastry brush, baste the corn liberally with the coco cream. Spread the crunchy topping on a baking sheet or large plate and roll the corn in the mix to apply. Alternatively, sprinkle with the crunchy topping. Garnish with chopped herbs and a squeeze of lime juice. Sink your teeth in and enjoy!

A Word on Ceviche

In its simplest form, ceviche is fresh, raw seafood quickly marinated in an acid, such as lime juice, and salt until "cooked." Through this process, the proteins in the seafood are "denatured"—texturally transformed by the citric acid present in the lime juice or other acid of your marinade. Denaturing also occurs when meat is cooked using fire or heat. The main difference is that heat kills bacteria, whereas acidic marinades cannot kill parasites or bacteria. Therefore, it is essential to prepare ceviche with the freshest seafood available.

Ceviche originated in Peru; whether its origins date to Incan, pre-Columbian, or post-colonial cultures is the topic of some debate. It is believed that the word "ceviche," or "sebiche" as it is commonly spelled in Latin America, comes from the Quechua word "siwiche," meaning "fresh fish" or "soft fish." The word also relates to the Spanish word "escabeche," which describes the process of marinating meat or fish in vinegar. In Peru, ceviche is marinated with sweet potato and corn on the cob; in Ecuador, it's served with a hearty portion of popcorn or patacones, crispy fried green plantains, on the side.

At the restaurant, we playfully reimagine ceviche on an almost-daily basis. We love to plug into the season's most exciting offerings, such as husk cherries, shiso leaves, chamomile, or tomato, leaving them in their original form or using them to flavor the agua that will serve as the base of our ceviche.

If ceviche were a piece of music, seafood is the melody, agua is the tempo, and the seasonal components are the harmony, all coming together in one glorious composition that quite literally sings while you eat it. The agua should be so delicious and seasoned so perfectly that you and your guests will want to drink the leftovers after the seafood has been gobbled up. At the restaurant, we often offer to pour the liquid from the plate into a shot glass, so guests can drink every last dropful. Take advantage of the seasons and be imaginative. Look in the forgotten corners of your fridge or countertop—got half an avocado and some celery? Enjoy the interplay of textures and flavors!

Here are some of our favorite ceviche recipes, which can be selected and paired with any choice of seafood, though we also provide suggestions for some of our most successful flavor combinations. The other elements of a ceviche—"the parts," as we'll refer to them—can be assembled from anything you like or have on hand. Crunchy, juicy, sweet, sour, or salty—you can have it all.

How to Choose Seafood

While it's convenient to choose a fillet at the seafood market, we recommend that you ask your fishmonger to break down a whole fish, as it is easier to gauge its freshness and quality. (Plus, you can make stock with the bones that same day or freeze them for up to a month, adding other bits and pieces, like shrimp shells, as you cook throughout the month.) When selecting a whole fish, look at the eyes—the less cloudy and filmy they are, the fresher the catch. And ask to look under the gills—bright red and pink coloring is best, and dull or gray coloring means that the fish is less likely to be fresh. If the catch of the day smells super "fishy," think twice before using it. Most of our recipes call for raw fish, so be sure to select high-quality seafood. Not all wild-caught fish is sustainable, and not all farmed fish is safely farmed, so do your research at the fish counter, and don't be afraid to ask questions. Monterey Bay Aquarium Seafood Watch is a good source of information about seafood safety and sustainability.

How to Butcher a Fish

This technique will work for most but not all fish; it works best with fish like sea bass, porgy, salmon, and tuna, which have a similar skeletal structure. Ask your fishmonger to scale and gut your fish. If you're feeling a little lost, remember that YouTube is your friend for fish butchering tutorials.

1. With the knife at a 45-degree angle, cut the fillet away from the head by slicing behind the head, gills, and collar bone.
2. With the knife blade pointing away from you, cut toward the head, along the back edge of the fish. Gently slide the knife along the rib bones, being careful not to lose any flesh, until you reach the center spine.
3. Repeat on the belly side, cutting across and then scraping along the rib bones until you reach the center spine.
4. With your knife just behind the collar bone, begin to lift the fillet by gently slicing the flesh along the spine, bone by bone.
5. Work all the way to the tail and remove from the carcass. Repeat steps 1 through 5 on the other side of the fish.
6. Examine the fillet and remove any pin bones, sinew, or belly fat.
7. To separate the skin from the fillet, grab the tail end of the fish and make an angled cut, away from you, between the flesh and the skin. Turn your blade parallel to the cutting board and begin to gently saw across, cutting the flesh away from the skin. As you run your blade along, hold the skin tight and pull it side to side. When the fillet is completely removed, inspect it and remove any skin that was left behind.
8. For ceviche, remove dark bloodlines or fibrous sinew. Cut against the grain into slices— the thinner the slice, the shorter the marinade time.
9. Again: watch pros showing off their skills on YouTube. That's what we like to do.

To Devein or Not to Devein?

This is a hot-button topic, so we are dissecting it for you here. When working with shrimp, you will notice a small red or black line running along the top edge. It is the vein, a nice word for saying intestines, or really, poop. Yes, the color is different based on what the shrimp ate. "Yuck," you might say. "I must remove it at once!" Au contraire. Going through all that labor is only important when eating shrimp raw, because it might harbor bacteria. If you're planning on cooking the shrimp, well then, it's really an aesthetic choice, and it depends on how lazy you're feeling. We will help you by indicating when it is necessary.

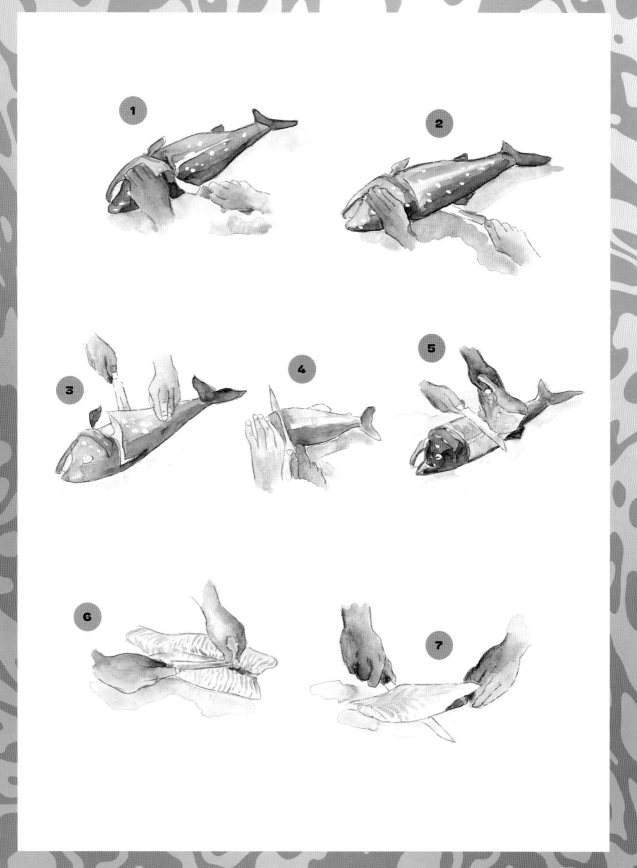

SCALLOP CRUDO WITH GREEN BANANA, COCONUT, AND DILL

Serves 2 to 4

Agua

One 12 oz can unsweetened full-fat coconut milk
Zest and juice of 2 limes
2 Tbsp fish sauce
Kosher salt

Crudo

½ lb dry-packed sea scallops
1 green banana (look for green tips)
2 Tbsp freshly squeezed lime juice, plus more as needed
1 Tbsp plus 1 tsp extra-virgin olive oil, plus more as needed
1 Fresno or other fresh red chile, minced
2 sprigs dill

We often play with ingredients that look like each other, so the eye begins a journey of disorientation before the food hits your taste buds. This dish simultaneously enchants and bewilders the palate. The green banana (look for green tips) and scallop, with similar textures and cut into the same size and shape, find a luxurious home in an unctuous, cold, and silky agua of coconut milk, lime juice, and fish sauce. Once you have a spoonful, you may wonder to yourself "What is banana? What is scallop?" But it does not matter, as you have slipped into a pool of sumptuous delight.

TO MAKE THE AGUA: In a small bowl, combine the coconut milk, lime zest and juice, and the fish sauce. Use an immersion blender or whisk to blend until homogenous and creamy. Cover and refrigerate until cool to the touch.

TO MAKE THE CRUDO: Pat dry the scallops with a paper towel. Remove and discard the "foot." Cut each scallop horizontally and then vertically to make ¼ to ½ in cubes. Peel the green banana then cut it to match the size and shape of the scallop pieces. In a medium bowl, combine cubed scallop and banana with 1 Tbsp of the lime juice and gently toss to combine. Cover and refrigerate for at least 20 minutes.

TO SERVE: Add the agua to the crudo and gently toss to coat. Add the remaining 1 Tbsp of lime juice and 1 Tbsp of the olive oil and season with salt. Taste it to make sure it's tangy and salty and add more lime juice, olive oil, or salt as needed. To plate, pile the banana-scallop mixture in the center of a serving dish. Sprinkle with the minced chile and drizzle with the remaining 1 tsp of olive oil. Pull the smallest sprigs of dill from the main stem to garnish the crudo. Enjoy right away.

A Little Acid Never Hurt Anyone

This creamy, silky dish begs for a bright, sharp vivacious wine. Acid in a wine is like conversation at a party—it's key to having a good time, but if there's too much or it's heavy-handed, it can leave you flinching. How, you ask, do I know if there's too much acid? Pay attention to where the wine hits you in the throat. Does it make your salivary glands hurt like you just ate a lemon? That's a lot of acid. Acid, when done right, is a fabulous team player in a wine, lending shape, edge, and brightness to your experience of flavor. When a wine has too much acid (also known as Volatile Acidity or VA), it can taste like orange juice at room temperature or smell like nail polish remover.

RAW SHRIMP IN TOMATO AND CHILE PEPPER AGUA

Serves 4

1 lb good quality shrimp,
    peeled, deveined, and
    cut lengthwise in half
Kosher salt
½ cup plus 2 Tbsp freshly
    squeezed lime juice
    (from 4 limes)
1 ripe, juicy tomato, halved
    and stem removed
1 or 2 fresh chiles, such
    as Fresno, jalapeño,
    serrano, or habanero

Quick Citrus Pickle for
    garnish (optional,
    page 41)

Tortilla chips, for serving
    (optional)

"Raw shrimp?" you might ask. "Yes, a thousand times yes!" we respond. Don't be afraid! Quickly cured by tart lime juice and salt, these shrimp are sweet, tender, and full of flavor. You'll find yourself surprised and refreshed by this delightful dish, bathed in a sea of piquant tomato agua. If you use habaneros, be careful—they are hot!

On a medium plate, season the shrimp with salt. Cover generously with 2 Tbsp of the lime juice, tossing gently to coat. Let marinate in the refrigerator for at least 30 minutes and up to 1 hour.

Meanwhile, in a blender, combine the tomato and the remaining ½ cup of lime juice. Blend to combine, while gradually adding the chiles to build the heat to your taste and seasoning with salt. Continue blending until smooth then push through a fine-mesh sieve, discarding any solids. Pour the liquid over the shrimp and gently toss to coat. Cover and refrigerate for 1 hour—the shrimp will turn slightly milky in color but not opaque.

TO SERVE: Garnish with pickled onions and enjoy solo or with tortilla chips on the side.

SALMON WITH DAIKON RADISH, CITRUS, AND CILANTRO STEM

Serves 2 to 4

1 small daikon radish, scrubbed and thinly sliced on a mandoline

Juice of 1 lime

Kosher salt

2 Tbsp finely chopped cilantro stems

½ jalapeño, finely minced

1 Tbsp extra-virgin olive oil

½ lb skinless sushi-grade salmon fillet (or tuna, scallops, or halibut)

1 small grapefruit, orange, or pomelo, cut into segments with the pith removed

Salmon is rarely featured in ceviche, but we love its fatty, buttery quality and the way it's enlivened by bright citrus juice. When selecting salmon, look for fish that's been sustainably harvested. With salmon ceviche we prefer to not marinate the fish in lime juice, because it is very quick to become a grayish color, but instead opt for a quick kissing of acid toward the end. The cilantro stem condiment, while oh-so-simple to make, delivers a flavorful punch, and we recommend stealing the concept for grilled steak or seared scallops.

In a non-metal bowl, combine the daikon radish slices, lime juice, and a pinch of salt. Toss to mix well. Let marinate in the refrigerator for at least 20 minutes and up to 1 hour.

Meanwhile, in a small bowl, combine the cilantro stems, jalapeño, and olive oil. Season with salt and set aside.

Carefully examine the salmon for pin bones and gently remove them with a tweezer. With your sharpest knife, held at a 45-degree angle, use smooth single cuts (no sawing!) to thinly slice the salmon into ¼ in slices. Sprinkle with a little salt.

TO SERVE: Artfully arrange the daikon radish slices, salmon slices, and grapefruit segments on a plate. Spoon the cilantro condiment on top. To eat, use your fingers to arrange one perfect bite composed of all the flavors.

CEVICHE MIXTO WITH POPCORN

Serves 6 to 8

Kosher salt
Peel of 1 orange plus 2
    cups freshly squeezed
    orange juice (from
    6 to 8 oranges)
2 Tbsp whole aromatic
    spices, such as
    a combination of
    coriander, cinnamon,
    and allspice
½ lb raw shrimp, peeled
    and deveined
½ lb baby octopus
½ lb skinless red snapper
    fillet (or any medium-
    firm saltwater fish)
½ cup chopped cilantro,
    stems and leaves
1 cup cubed watermelon
3 cups freshly squeezed
    lime juice (from 24
    limes)
1 small red onion, diced
1 jalapeño, finely minced
2 avocados, ripe but firm
Fragrant Chile Oil
    (page 38, optional)

Popcorn or plantain chips,
    for serving

This is our version of the classic ceviche that is sold in beachside cabanas all over South and Central America. The agua is a balancing act of flavors, so please use your judgment. If it feels too acidic, add a little more salt! If octopus is hard to find in your area, use extra shrimp and fish. This recipe can be made a day in advance.

In a medium bowl, make an ice bath of half ice and half water. Fill a medium pot with generously salted water (it should taste like the ocean). Add the orange peel and aromatic spices and bring to a roaring boil. Drop in the shrimp and poach, immediately turning off the heat. Hold in the water until pink on the outside and just barely cooked on the inside, 45 seconds to 1 minute. Using a spider or slotted spoon, immediately plunge the shrimp into the ice bath; reserve the poaching liquid. Once cool, drain the shrimp and pat dry with a paper towel. Cut into ½ in pieces, put in a bowl, cover, and refrigerate while you cook the octopus.

Return the poaching liquid to a boil. Drop in the baby octopus and poach until easily pierceable with a knife, 30 to 45 minutes. Set aside on a resting rack to cool.

Meanwhile, remove any sinew or darker patches from the snapper fillet, and cut into ½ in cubes.

In a large non-metal bowl, combine the orange and lime juice and season with salt. Taste it and adjust until tangy and bright from the lime, with a background of sweetness from the orange. Add the red onion, jalapeño, watermelon, avocado, shrimp, octopus, snapper, and most of the cilantro. Gently toss to combine. Cover and refrigerate for 30 minutes. Taste the ceviche. The flavor of the seafood will have started to permeate the agua, as its juices are released. If you think it could use more flavor development, allow it to sit in the fridge for another 30 minutes. Right before serving, add a dash of lime juice and season with a little extra salt.

TO SERVE: Sprinkle the ceviche with the reserved cilantro and a drizzle of chile oil. Serve with a side of popcorn or plantain chips.

SHRIMP COCKTAIL WITH NIMBU KA ACHAR COCKTAIL SAUCE

Serves 4 to 6

Shrimp

¼ cup granulated sugar
2 Tbsp kosher salt
1 orange, quartered
1 yellow onion, quartered
½ bunch cilantro
4 cloves
1 lb medium or large
   shrimp, peeled and
   deveined

Cocktail Sauce

One 15 oz can whole
   peeled or chopped
   tomatoes
¼ cup nimbu ka achar
1 tsp Chile Vinegar
   (page 39) or hot
   sauce, such as
   Tabasco or Crystal
½ tsp fish sauce
¼ tsp Worcestershire sauce
Juice of 2 limes
2 garlic cloves
Kosher salt

For Serving

3 Tbsp Pickled Mustard
   Seeds (page 44)
1 lime, cut into wedges
A few sprigs of cilantro
Fragrant Chile Oil
   (page 38)

This is a classic shrimp cocktail with a twist. Instead of horseradish, we use nimbu ka achar, or Indian lime pickle—whole limes rubbed in salt and spices and fermented in sunlight. We're *obsessed* with this flavor-packed, pungent condiment, and always order extra when dining at our local Indian restaurant (order some to-go!). The salt, acid, and bitterness combined with the floral essence of the limes pairs perfectly with the tomato and sweet poached shrimp to make the dish sing.

TO MAKE THE SHRIMP: In a large stockpot, combine 8 cups of water with the sugar, salt, orange, onion, cilantro, and cloves. Bring to a boil, stirring occasionally to dissolve the sugar and salt. In a medium bowl, make an ice bath of half ice and half water. Once the water has come to a boil, drop in the shrimp, turn off the heat, cover, and let stand until the shrimp are plump, pink, and juicy, but not too tightly curled, about 3 minutes. Immediately plunge the shrimp into the ice bath. Drain and pat dry with a paper towel. Refrigerate until ready to serve.

TO MAKE THE COCKTAIL SAUCE: In a blender, combine the tomatoes, nimbu ka achar, chile vinegar, fish sauce, Worcestershire sauce, lime juice, and garlic and blend until smooth. Season with salt. Refrigerate until ready to serve.

TO SERVE: Arrange the shrimp in an elegant manner on a serving platter. Garnish with pickled mustard seeds, lime wedges, cilantro, and a drizzle of chile oil never hurt anybody. Serve with the cocktail sauce alongside.

TUNA TATAKI WITH CONCORD GRAPE NUOC CHAM AND SHISO

Serves 2 to 4

Seared Tuna

½ lb sushi-grade raw tuna
    loin, preferably a long,
    narrow piece
Kosher salt
1 Tbsp canola oil

Nuoc Cham

1 cup Concord or red
    grapes
Zest of 4 limes
½ cup lime juice
3 Tbsp fish sauce
3 garlic cloves, minced
1 shallot
1 fresh serrano chile,
    minced (keep seeds)
¼ cup extra-virgin olive oil
Sugar as needed

Garnish

12 shiso leaves (or Thai
    or regular basil leaves)
Crispy Garlic Chips
    (page 37)
Flaky finishing salt, such
    as Maldon
Extra-virgin olive oil

The Japanese word "tataki" has two meanings. The first refers to meat or fish that is seared on the outside and raw on the inside. The second definition comes from the verb "tataku," meaning "to pound" or "to hammer." We use both methods. We sear the tuna, and we smash the grapes, then use their skin, juice, and flesh as the base of a nuoc cham, a classic Vietnamese dipping sauce. The garlic chips process is a lengthy one, but we promise the end results are oh so worth it! They add a necessary crunch and depth of flavor that is worth the time and effort; make them a day ahead to spread out your labor!

TO MAKE THE TUNA: Season the tuna with salt on all sides. In a medium nonstick skillet over medium-high heat, warm the oil. Add the tuna and quickly sear it, turning it to sear each side for about 1 minute—it should be slightly crispy and golden brown outside and remain raw inside. Put the tuna on a baking sheet and refrigerate immediately.

TO MAKE THE NUOC CHAM: Working in batches, use a mortar and pestle to pound the grapes. Transfer to a medium bowl. (If you hate grape seeds, you can attempt to remove them. If you don't mind a little crunch (and extra nutrition), leave them in!) Add the lime zest and juice, fish sauce, garlic, shallot, and serrano chile, whisking in the olive oil at the end. Taste the sauce. Does it need more salt? Add fish sauce. Does it need to be brighter? Add lime juice. If the grapes are more sour than sweet, add a tiny bit of sugar—we'll let you decide.

TO SERVE: Arrange the shiso leaves so they are slightly overlapping on a serving platter. Using a sharp knife, gently and evenly cut the tuna crosswise into ¼ in slices. Place the tuna on top of the shiso leaves then generously sauce each slice with the nuoc cham. Top each slice of tuna with a slice of crispy garlic. Sprinkle with flaky salt and drizzle with olive oil. Enjoy immediately, using a shiso leaf as the wrap for each slice of tuna. Faint from pleasure!

AVOCADO SALAD

Serves 2 to 4

Vinaigrette

2 garlic cloves, peeled
2 tsp kosher salt
¾ cup freshly squeezed
  lime juice
1 cup canola oil

Salad

1 head iceberg lettuce
1 ripe avocado
One 12 oz can hearts
  of palm, cut into
  ¼ in rounds
¼ red onion, thinly sliced
¼ cup toasted pepitas
Flaky finishing salt, such
  as Maldon

We didn't invent this salad, nor is it "ours" to claim. It's served—sometimes with tomato, sometimes without—in taco stands, pupuserias, and beachside bars all over the world. When we were planning our first menu, we knew we wanted to have a super fresh iceberg salad. In the age of farm-to-table madness, people love to hate on iceberg lettuce and relegate it to low-class diner and salad bar fare, but we just tell them, "We like to eat our water." Iceberg delivers the best crunch and it contains so much water that you really do feel refreshed after eating it. You'll likely have a bit of leftover dressing, which is a good thing—this versatile vinaigrette will keep in your fridge for a week or two. Get creative and use it to marinate shrimp or chicken, or even add some to tuna salad! If you don't have a mortar and pestle (you should!), finely mince the garlic and combine it with the salt, lime juice, and oil in a jar then cover and shake!

TO MAKE THE VINAIGRETTE: With a mortar and pestle, smash the garlic and salt to form a smooth paste. Gradually whisk in the lime juice a few droplets at a time. Gradually add the oil in a slow, steady stream, whisking to emulsify. Leftovers can be stored in a jar for up to 1 week.

TO MAKE THE SALAD: Cut the iceberg lettuce into large wedges and arrange on a serving platter. Drizzle some vinaigrette into the grooves of each wedge. Cut the avocado in half, remove the pit, and put each side face-down on a cutting board. Carefully peel back the skin without bruising the tops of the avocado halves. Use a small, sharp knife to cut slices from near the belly button to the bottom of each half. Press lightly on the avocado halves, directing the pressure toward one side to separate and fan the slices. Place the avocado fans and heart of palm rounds on the iceberg wedges and drizzle with more vinaigrette. Sprinkle with red onion, pepitas, and a little flaky salt and serve immediately.

CELERY CAESAR SALAD

Serves 3 to 5

Dressing

1 cup freshly grated
    Parmesan cheese
2 Tbsp fish sauce
1 Tbsp freshly ground
    black pepper
6 garlic cloves, peeled
Zest and juice of 3 lemons
2 large egg yolks
2 Tbsp ice water
1 cup extra-virgin olive oil
Kosher salt

Salad

½ small white onion, thinly
    sliced on a mandoline
1 celery head, stalks and
    leaves separated and
    thoroughly washed
Kosher salt and freshly
    ground black pepper
¼ cup capers, chopped
¼ cup toasted pistachios,
    chopped
½ lemon
¼ cup freshly grated
    Parmesan cheese

One of the best salads ever invented, the Caesar needs no introduction. It's also a top contender for our "last meal on earth." Veering from tradition, we make ours with crisp, juicy celery, tons of lemon zest, and fish sauce (instead of anchovies). The briny pop of the capers and crunch of the pistachios round it out and give it a playful mouthfeel. Consider eating this salad with a spoon to scoop up all the saucy bits. The recipe makes 2 cups of dressing, so there will be leftovers, but it keeps for up to a week in the fridge.

TO MAKE THE DRESSING: In a blender, combine the Parmesan, fish sauce, pepper, garlic, lemon zest and juice, and egg yolks. Pulse to combine. Gradually add the oil, followed by the ice water, in a slow, steady stream, blending until emulsified, about 4 minutes. Add salt or acid as needed—you're in charge of your flavor destiny! Store in an airtight container in the refrigerator for up to a week.

TO MAKE THE SALAD: Put the thinly sliced onion in a small bowl, cover with ice water, and let stand for 10 minutes to soften the bite. Strain and set aside.

    Cut the celery stalks on the bias into roughly ⅛ in thick slices. (If wilted, the cut celery can be soaked in an ice water bath for 10 minutes and dried before dressing.) Put the celery in a large bowl, season with salt, and toss to combine. Add the onion, capers, and most of the pistachios and toss again. Spoon ¼ cup of the dressing into the bowl and squeeze in the juice from the half lemon for an extra burst of acid. Toss and season with salt as needed.

TO SERVE: Using a large spoon, arrange the salad in an elegant, central stack on a serving platter—it should be wide at the base but still have good height. Sprinkle with Parmesan, celery leaves, and the remaining pistachios. Season with pepper. Enjoy this heaping pile of flavor with your friends.

LETTUCES WITH HIPPIE MUSTARD DRESSING

Serves 2 to 4

Vinaigrette

1 cup nutritional yeast
½ cup Dijon mustard
½ cup ají amarillo paste
Zest and juice of 3 lemons
1 Tbsp freshly ground
      black pepper
2 tsp ground turmeric
3 garlic cloves, minced
½ cup extra-virgin olive oil
Kosher salt

Crunchy Topping

1 Tbsp sunflower seeds,
      chopped
1 Tbsp flax seeds
1 tsp chia seeds
1 tsp smoked paprika
½ tsp kosher salt

Salad

½ lb mixed lettuces, such
      as butterhead, romaine,
      red leaf, and mizuna
2 cups mixed fresh herbs,
      such as mint, tarragon,
      dill, cilantro, lovage,
      parsley, and chervil—
      truly anything goes!
Edible flowers, such as
      nasturtium, violas, or
      borage (optional, for
      extra flair)

At our pandemic summer pop-up, Fuego 69, we described our food as "zing-zang, frisky-fresh, hyper-local, wood-fired, pescatarian hippie," an intentional jumble of applicable jargon that is just our style. This vinaigrette reminds us of sunny summer days when we strip down to the bare essentials and our mouths water in anticipation of the season's freshest bounty. But this vinaigrette is good year-round, especially in the dead of winter, when a moment of brightness is needed. Loaded with protein, vitamins, and minerals, nutritional yeast is good for you (it's also vegan—shhhh!) and its cheesy umami flavor is delicious, too. Use leftovers for any salad, or as a marinade for chicken or fish.

TO MAKE THE VINAIGRETTE: In a medium bowl, whisk together the nutritional yeast, mustard, ají amarillo paste, lemon zest and juice, pepper, turmeric, and garlic. Gradually add the olive oil in a slow, steady stream, whisking until emulsified. Season with salt and store in an airtight container for up to a week.

TO MAKE THE CRUNCHY TOPPING: In a small bowl, combine the sunflower seeds, flax seeds, chia seeds, smoked paprika, and salt. Store in an airtight container for up to a month.

TO MAKE THE SALAD: Spread a large spoonful of the vinaigrette in the bottom of a large bowl. Add the lettuces and herbs, and use your hands to gently toss them, treating the fragile lettuces with love and kindness and making sure they are deliciously and lightly dressed in vinaigrette. Arrange on a serving platter, sprinkle generously with the crunchy topping, and garnish with edible flowers. Eat with your fingers while wearing next to nothing.

HEIRLOOM TOMATOES WITH PEANUT SALSA MACHA

Serves 2 to 4

Peanut Salsa Macha

10 dates
1 cup crushed roasted
　　and salted peanuts
¾ cup red wine vinegar
¾ cup extra-virgin olive oil
½ cup Fragrant Chile Oil
　　(page 38)
3 Tbsp cacao nibs
　　(optional, but why
　　opt out?)
2 Tbsp cacao powder
1 Tbsp granulated sugar
2 garlic cloves, minced
2 tsp kosher salt
1 tsp freshly ground
　　black pepper

Salad

4 ripe heirloom tomatoes
Coarse salt
Fresh dill

Summer comes late in Upstate New York, and so does tomato season. When it finally hits, usually at the end of July, dopamine immediately rushes to our brains and there's little else that compares. Tomatoes for breakfast, tomatoes on toast, tomato and mayo sandwiches, tomato cocktails, and of course, tomato salads! While a perfectly ripe tomato does a lot of the work in this salad, it is not to be outdone by the salsa macha, an incredible sauce and a Lil' Deb's staple, as well as a strong example of colonialism's impact on global foodways. It combines ingredients native to Mexico, where the sauce originates, like cacao, chocolate, and chiles, and two key ingredients brought to the Americas by colonizers: red wine vinegar and olive oil. Spicy, umami, slick, sweet, and pungent, it is an unforgettable sauce. Feel free to add other seasonal veggies like cucumber or radish. This is a case in which anything goes, as the salsa macha does all the work for you. We also love to snack on celery sticks filled with salsa macha, because its nostalgic flavor profile takes us back to our "ants on a log" days.

TO MAKE THE SALSA MACHA: Remove the pits from the dates and thinly slice. In a medium bowl, whisk together the peanuts, red wine vinegar, olive oil, chile oil, cacao nibs, cacao powder, sugar, dates, garlic, salt, and pepper. Refrigerate in an airtight container for up to 1 month.

TO MAKE THE SALAD: Cut the tomatoes into rounds, somewhere between thin and thick, so they hold their steak-like shape. Arrange the tomato slices on a serving platter and drizzle liberally with a hearty portion of the salsa macha. Sprinkle with the coarse salt and fresh dill and serve.

Pro Tip

Tomatoes are best kept out of direct sunlight and at room temperature. Resist the temptation to refrigerate them, as the cooler temperature decreases their fructose content, reducing the intensity of their natural flavors, and causes their cells to rupture, making them mealy :(

UMEBOSHI PURPLE POTATO ESCABECHE

Serves 2 to 4

Salad

2 lbs purple fingerling
  potatoes, peeled
2 Tbsp kosher salt
1 Tbsp red wine vinegar
1 large or a handful
  of small, in season
  peppers of any
  color, thinly sliced
1 carrot, cut into
  thin rounds
¼ red onion, thinly sliced
1 cup husk cherries,
  halved, or 2 tomatillos,
  cut into rounds
Juice of 1 lime, for finishing

Vinaigrette

¼ cup umeboshi vinegar
¼ cup red wine vinegar
2 Tbsp fresh oregano
½ tsp freshly ground
  black pepper
2 garlic cloves, minced
¾ cup extra virgin olive oil
½ cup Fragrant Chile Oil
  (page 38)

Year after year, when purple potatoes come into season, we are hit with the same sense of awe that their vibrant color exists in nature. These potatoes scream luxury with their pillowy texture. If you can't find potatoes that are purple inside and out, Yukon Golds, yellow or white fingerlings, or red bliss will do. Just remember: This dish is meant to highlight the gorgeous colors of early fall. We also love including husk cherries, which have a mysterious flavor and a punchiness that provides pops of sweet juiciness throughout the dish. Umeboshi vinegar, made from salted and pickled plums, is your secret ingredient here. It packs a serious hit of salty, tangy notes, so you'll want to balance it out with lots of olive oil and lime juice and hold back on adding extra salt.

Fun Fact: The origin of the word "escabeche" is Persian; the dish was brought to Spain by the Moors and from there spread to Spanish colonies around the world, from the Philippines to the Caribbean. Each iteration is different, with the common thread being food cooked and marinated in vinegar. In Mexico, escabeche refers to a classic condiment of pickled jalapeños and vegetables, whereas if you order escabeche in the Catalan region of Spain, you'd be served fried fish marinated in vinegar and peppers, a bit like Jamaican escovitch.

TO MAKE THE SALAD: In a medium stockpot, cover the potatoes with water, season with the salt, and bring to a boil. Continue boiling until fork tender, about 20 minutes. Immediately remove the potatoes from the water and put on a baking sheet. Drizzle with the red wine vinegar and gently toss to coat. Cut the potatoes into rounds and set aside.

TO MAKE THE VINAIGRETTE: In a small bowl, whisk together the umeboshi vinegar, red wine vinegar, oregano, pepper, and garlic. Gradually add the olive oil and chile oil in a slow, steady stream, whisking until emulsified. Taste! The mixture should be fairly salty and bright, with a deep funky heat from the chile oil permeating throughout. Store in an airtight container and refrigerate for up to a week.

TO SERVE: Toss the potatoes with the pepper, carrot, onion, and husk cherries. Add a generous amount of the vinaigrette and toss to coat. Squeeze lime juice over the salad for extra brightness. Taste and adjust the seasoning as needed. It's delicious served warm or cooled.

ENDIVES WITH MINT, SHRIMP POWDER, AND ORANGE BLOSSOM VINAIGRETTE

Serves 2 to 4

Shrimp Powder

½ cup dried shrimp
2 cups hot water

Vinaigrette

3 garlic cloves, peeled
1 tsp kosher salt
Zest and juice of 1 orange
1 tsp red pepper flakes
    or the sludge at the
    bottom of your Fragrant
    Chile Oil (page 38)
Juice of 2 limes
1 Tbsp fish sauce
1 tsp orange blossom water
½ tsp vanilla paste or seeds
    from 1 vanilla bean pod
¾ cup extra-virgin olive oil

Salad

4 heads endive
¼ cup mint leaves

We will shout it from the rooftops: We love eating with our fingers! And if there's one salad that begs to be consumed sans fork, this is it. Feathery shrimp floss made from dried, rehydrated shrimp creates soft pillows when intermingled with a vinaigrette that has a heavenly vanilla kiss. Crisp, bitter endive acts as the perfect vehicle to scoop it all up. Before plating, first think about your salad's architecture—consider the Fibonacci sequence and cascading dominoes. Eat now, regret nothing. Use leftover shrimp powder to give umami richness to stocks, add to salsa macha (page 113) for depth of flavor, or sprinkle on larb (page 143) or charred cabbage (page 139).

TO MAKE THE SHRIMP POWDER: In a medium bowl, soak the dried shrimp in hot water for 20 minutes. Strain and pat dry between paper towels. Transfer to a food processor and pulse until a rough powder takes form. Use right away to make this salad or store in an airtight container in the refrigerator for up to 1 month.

TO MAKE THE VINAIGRETTE: In a mortar and pestle, pound the garlic and salt into a smooth paste. Add the orange zest and red pepper flakes and pound a few times to incorporate. Whisk in the orange juice and lime juice, the fish sauce, orange blossom water, and vanilla paste. Gradually add the olive oil in a slow, steady stream, whisking until emulsified. Stir vigorously before serving.

TO MAKE THE SALAD: Arrange a few endive sections in a circular pattern on a serving platter. Drizzle with some of the vinaigrette and sprinkle with a bit of mint. Repeat this process, building each layer in tighter and tighter circles, and add a generous sprinkling of shrimp powder to finish. Eat now (with your fingers), regret nothing.

PINEAPPLE AMBROSIA

Serves 2 to 4

½ ripe pineapple,
quartered, cut into thin
half moons, and chilled
1 watermelon radish,
peeled and cut into
thin rounds
1 avocado, cut in half and
sliced into half moons
Zest and juice of ½ lime
1 tsp extra-virgin olive oil
1 tsp Lemon Verbena Salt
(page 35)
Cotija cheese, for serving

We love the name of this salad, because it reminds us of the ambrosia of the Greek gods and makes us feel immortal. It's sweet and bitter, with just a hint of funk—add in our Lemon Verbena Salt and feel the other ingredients sing in celestial harmony—and thoroughly unrelated to the Jell-O salad of the 1950s. Think of this as a very refreshing savory fruit salad because it is. Enjoy it for breakfast, at snack time, on the beach, or as a side salad with dinner.

On a serving platter, arrange the pineapple, watermelon radish, and avocado in scalloped layers by overlapping each item slightly, in alternating rows in a single layer. Drizzle with lime zest and juice and olive oil and sprinkle with the lemon verbena salt. Use a Microplane to grate cotija over the salad. Serve cold.

How to Choose a Wine with Your Meal (It Might Not Be A-Pair-Ant)

We are steadfast believers in drinking whatever wine you want, at whatever time you want. However, we also believe that you should love what you want to love, and if wine pairings are what you love, who are we to stop you? When pairing a wine with a dish, you can explore two types of pairing relationships: parallel and perpendicular. You can pair a wine that mirrors and emphasizes the flavors of your food, or you can pair a wine that contrasts and intersects with those flavors. An example of a parallel pairing with salsa macha (see page 113) would be a light but earthy red with nice acid because the weight and character of the wine echoes the weight and character of the meal. There are two directions for a perpendicular pairing for salsa macha. One way would be to contrast the aromatics and earthiness of the cacao, peanut, and chile with an electric-dry white with zippy personality like the Trossen Riesling from the German Mosel Valley, a wine that's been described as "liquid cocaine." Another approach would be to amplify the delicate fruit of the tomatoes by selecting a wine with deeper tannins, creating contrast. Choose your fighter carefully and the world is your oyster!

"WHAT'S IN THE FRIDGE" CHEF'S TIGER SALAD

Serves 2

1 or 2 large eggs
½ cucumber, striped, cut
    lengthwise, seeds
    scooped, and sliced
    on a bias
½ hot fresh chile, such
    as jalapeño or serrano,
    seeded and thinly sliced
1 shallot, shaved into
    thin rounds
Kosher salt
1 Tbsp rice vinegar
1 tsp freshly squeezed
    lime juice
1 carrot, peeled and
    julienned
2 scallions, thinly sliced
    on a long bias
1 celery stalk, thinly sliced
    on a long bias
Mint leaves, roughly
    chopped
Parsley leaves and tender
    stems, roughly chopped
Cilantro leaves and tender
    stems, roughly chopped
1 tsp Fragrant Chile Oil
    (page 38)
1 Tbsp toasted sesame oil
Sesame seeds

This is more of a life philosophy than a recipe. It's about appreciating the vegetables that are wilting in the crisper drawer of your fridge on a random Wednesday night when you're saying to yourself, "I have *nothing* to make *anything* with and I *don't* want to go out to eat!" We are here to tell you that you *do* have everything you need. With a little love, ice water, and tender knife skills, you can turn wilting refrigerator misfits into a mouthwatering, satisfying salad. This recipe loosely combines the Northern Chinese tiger salad, or lao hu cai, which we love for its fresh flavor and bountiful use of herbs and chiles, and the North American chef's salad, which has an "everything but the kitchen sink" sensibility. You could add protein like chicken, shrimp, or tofu for a complete meal. Remember: if you don't have parsley, but you have dill, use it! If you don't have celery, but you have fennel, use it! Don't have a lime, use vinegar! Don't have eggs but have a can of sardines or a tin of tuna, use it! Poached chicken would be great in this! Don't be afraid to experiment! Make use of what you do have! Waste not, want not!

Bring a small pot of water to a boil. Using a ladle, slowly lower in the egg or eggs and cook for 9 minutes—for a softer egg, cook for 8 minutes. Run the egg under cold water to stop the cooking process. After it cools completely, peel, slice and set aside.

In a large bowl, add the cucumber, chile, and shallot. Season with salt, add the rice vinegar and lime juice, and toss to coat. Set aside to make a quick pickle.

In a large bowl, combine the carrot, scallions, celery, mint, parsley, and cilantro. Add 1 tsp of salt, the chile oil, and sesame oil and gently toss to coat. Add the cumber mixture and gently toss again. Add the sliced egg to the top of your salad, garnish with sesame seeds, and serve immediately.

CHAPTER FOUR

AROUSAL

EXPANDING TECHNIQUES TO TAKE THINGS TO THE NEXT LEVEL

RECIPES

We've held hands, gone on a couple of dates, even kissed a little, and we are very much enjoying your company—we hope you are enjoying ours too! The recipes to this point have been smaller bites. We're not fans of defined labels—for food *or* people—and often struggle to divide our menu into appetizers and entrées, because that's not how we like to eat, and our food often blurs those lines. While many of our dishes could easily float between one category or the other, this chapter focuses on recipes that are a little more involved, or slightly more filling. They are recipes that will nourish and strengthen the foundation of our growing relationship. If pressed, we'd call them main courses. We're ready to take things to the next level. Join us!

TEPPER'S FLATBREAD

Serves 8 to 10

Miso Tahini Spread

¼ cup barley miso
½ cup sesame tahini
1 cup thinly sliced scallions

Dough

1 Tbsp active dry yeast
2½ cups all-purpose flour
2⅓ cups buckwheat flour,
  plus more for rolling
2 to 2½ cups whole milk
  yogurt, plus extra as
  needed
½ tsp buckwheat honey
4 tsp kosher salt

For serving

Radishes, thinly sliced
Pickled onions
Fresh herbs
Sesame seeds

Tepper is a wonderful chef and steadfast friend, who is especially passionate about working with dough. Through their pop-up project, Circles, a "postmodern, transgender, circular experience," Tepper explores their obsession with pizza, bagels, and doughnuts. For our outdoor wood-fired concept, Fuego 69, we asked them to develop a flatbread dough using buckwheat flour, which we love for its complex flavor and nutritional value.

TO MAKE THE MISO TAHINI SPREAD: Combine the miso, tahini, and 2 Tbsp of water and stir vigorously until fully incorporated. Stir in the scallions and store in a container in the refrigerator for up to 1 month.

TO MAKE THE DOUGH: Bloom the yeast in 2 tbsp warm water for 1 minute. Next, in a large bowl, whisk together the all-purpose flour, buckwheat flour, and bloomed yeast. Add all of the yogurt and the honey and mix by hand or in a stand mixer with a dough hook on low speed for 30 seconds, and then turn it up to medium, mixing until a shaggy dough forms. Knead until the dough forms a unified ball. If it's too dry and not coming together, gradually add more yogurt, 1 tsp at a time. Place in a clean bowl, cover with plastic wrap, and let rest for 10 minutes in a warm place.

Add the salt and knead by hand or in a stand mixer with the dough hook attachment on low until the salt is incorporated and the dough ball is smooth, about 5 minutes. Cover the dough with a kitchen towel and let rest in a warm place until doubled in size, 1 to 2 hours. The dough should become softer and airier as it rises.

Divide the dough into 6 to 7 oz portions. On a work surface lightly dusted with buckwheat flour, roll out each portion into a 6 in round that's about ¼ in thick. Stack the flatbreads between parchment paper.

Set a rack in the middle of the oven and preheat the oven to 350°F. Put a baking sheet on the middle rack.

Heat a large cast-iron pan over medium-high heat. Put a flatbread in the center and cook until bubbles start to form on top and the flatbread starts to puff up, 2 to 3 minutes. Check the bottom to make sure it's browned but not charred then flip and cook the other side for another 2 to 3 minutes. Keep warm in the oven while you cook the remaining flatbread.

TO SERVE: Shmear flatbread with large spoonful of spread. Garnish with radishes, pickled onions, fresh herbs, and sesame seeds. Eat immediately.

CARMEN'S PÃO DE QUEIJO

**Serves a party!
(about 30 mini
rolls)**

4 cups tapioca flour
1 Tbsp anise seed
1 tsp kosher salt
1 cup whole milk
1 cup vegetable oil,
    plus more as needed
    for oiling hands
5 large eggs
2 cups freshly grated
    Parmesan cheese

Carmen is unforgettable! She is a brilliant Leo, who shines her light on anyone who needs it. In her role as a prep cook she brings warmth, thoughtfulness, and unhinged silliness to our kitchen. She is proudly from the Bahia region of Brazil and often cooks homegrown dishes, including these little cheesy rolls, which are among our favorite gluten-free snacks. Variations on pão de queijo, also called pan de yuca, can be found in Paraguay, Ecuador, Columbia, and the Dominican Republic, and they are often served as a quick, satisfying breakfast. We use Parmesan for its umami saltiness, but the type of cheese varies by region. You can try other cheeses too, like mozzarella or Cheddar. The dough can be frozen to have on hand for breakfast, snacks, or dinner and can be baked straight from the freezer—just add 5 minutes to the oven time.

Preheat the oven to 350°F.

In a large bowl, whisk together the tapioca flour, anise seed, and salt.

In a medium saucepan, bring the milk, vegetable oil, and 1 cup of water oil to a boil. Add to the tapioca mixture and carefully mix until fully combined. Let cool to room temperature.

Fill a small bowl with about ¼ cup of vegetable oil and line a baking sheet with parchment.

In a small bowl, whisk the eggs. Add to the room temperature tapioca mixture and combine by hand to form a sticky dough. Add the Parmesan cheese in three equal parts, continuing to mix with your hands until a soft dough forms.

With a medium spoon, scoop dough into roughly golf ball–sized portions, and with well-oiled hands, smooth and shape the dough into round buns—there should be about 30. Arrange on the parchment-lined baking sheet and bake until puffed up and lightly golden brown, 20 to 25 minutes (add 5 minutes if baking from frozen). Let cool for 5 minutes—no one wants a burnt tongue!—and serve warm.

LLAPINGACHOS WITH PEANUT SALSA AND PICKLES

Serves 10

Llapingachos

2½ lbs Yukon Gold
    potatoes, peeled
Kosher salt
1 Tbsp achiote paste
    (see page 188)
½ lb Muenster cheese,
    grated
3 scallions, thinly sliced
Neutral oil, for frying

Peanut Sauce

½ cup whole milk
¼ cup unsweetened
    peanut butter
1½ tsp achiote paste
    (see page 188)
1½ tsp light brown sugar
1 tsp kosher salt
1 small orange

Pickle Slaw

1 cup diced pineapple
1 to 2 radishes, shaved
    into half moons
½ red onion, cut into
    half moons
Zest and juice of 2 limes
1 tsp Aleppo pepper
Kosher salt
2 Tbsp mint leaves
2 Tbsp cilantro leaves

Eggs

Neutral oil, for frying
10 large eggs
Fragrant Chile Oil (page
    38), for garnish

Handed down by Carla's great-aunt Tia Rosario, via Carla's grandmother, Inés, this recipe for Ecuadorian potato pancakes with crispy fried eggs has been reinterpreted by us. It is a dish to be eaten in a living room, among cousins and friends and grandchildren, with everyone balancing a plate in their lap. Invite your friends over and serve them these llapingachos (pronounced "ya-pin-ga-choz") in all their crisp and gooey glory.

TO MAKE THE LLAPINGACHOS: In a stockpot, cover the potatoes with cold water. Season generously with salt and bring to a boil over high heat. Turn the heat to medium and simmer until fork tender, 20 to 30 minutes. Immediately strain and let cool slightly before handling (but don't wait too long, cold potatoes become gummy and hard to work with). Transfer to a large bowl, add the achiote paste, and mash to incorporate into the potatoes. Season with salt. Set aside to cool slightly but still remain warm.

In a small bowl, combine the Muenster and scallions.

Scoop the dough into roughly tennis ball–sized portions and use your hands to shape the dough into round balls—there should be about 10. Use your thumb to make an indentation in the center of each ball and then add about 1 Tbsp of the cheese and scallion mixture and use your fingers to wrap the dough around the filling and seal it inside the dough. Use your hands to flatten the balls into roughly 3 in rounds that are about ¾ in thick.

TO MAKE THE PEANUT SAUCE: In a blender, combine the milk, peanut butter, achiote paste, brown sugar, salt, and orange (zest, juice, and flesh). Blend until smooth.

TO MAKE THE PICKLE SLAW: In a small bowl, combine the pineapple, radishes, and red onion. Add the lime zest and juice, Aleppo pepper, and a pinch of salt and toss to combine.

TO FRY THE LLAPINGACHOS AND EGGS: Preheat the oven to 300°F.

Warm a large frying pan over medium-low heat. Lightly coat the cooking surface with 2 Tbsp of the neutral oil. Once hot, add the llapingachos in batches (wipe down the pan and add 2 Tbsp oil between each batch), evenly spaced, to the pan, and cook until the bottom has browned and formed a thin crust, 6 to 8 minutes. Flip and cook the other side for about 2 minutes then use a spatula to press down lightly. If cheese begins to ooze, you're getting close! Continue cooking until the other side is browned and crusty, 4 to 6 minutes. Don't be afraid to let it get crispy as it oozes—the cheese crust is one of the best parts. Keep warm in the oven while you cook the rest of the llapingachos.

Lightly coat a pan with oil; fry the eggs sunny side up, with a runny yolk.

"I'm so happy you're getting
Muenster. Everybody forgets
about Muenster, nobody cares
about Muenster, but it's such
a good cheese."
—ShopRite Deli Lady

TO SERVE: Arrange the llapingachos on a serving platter and drizzle with peanut sauce. Place a fried egg on top of each llapingacho. Add the mint and cilantro to the pickle salad, toss to combine, and add a small spoonful to each llapingacho. Drizzle chile oil over everything. Devour.

CURED TROUT

Serves 4 to 6

1 lb skin-on trout or
    salmon fillet
1 Tbsp granulated sugar
3 Tbsp Lemon Verbena
    Salt (page 35)

Though simple to prepare, this recipe will impress your guests, because there's nothing more low-key cool than laying out a gorgeous piece of fish and casually saying, "Oh yeah, I cured it myself." Curing is an age-old process of preserving proteins that doesn't require advanced skills, just salt, sugar, and time. Our recipe uses one of our favorite herbs, lemon verbena, because its floral flavor pairs so well with the fish. Served with bagels or toast, this dish is a great stand-in for traditional gravlax. We serve ours alongside warm, boiled buttery potatoes, thinly sliced raw onion, and a few lemon wedges.

With a clean cloth or paper towel, pat dry both sides of the fish.

In a small bowl, combine the sugar and lemon verbena salt and sprinkle generously on both sides of the fish. Gently wrap the fish in plastic wrap and arrange, skin side down, on a baking sheet. Put a second baking sheet on top of the fish then put cans or a heavy pan on top to gently weigh down the fish. Refrigerate for 12 hours then flip the fish over, put the baking sheet and cans back on top, and refrigerate for 12 more hours.

Unwrap the fish and cut off a thin slice. Taste for salt. If the flavor is just right for you, then it is good to go. If it's too intense, rinse the trout under cold water. Pat the fish dry all over with a paper towel and let air dry in the refrigerator for a few hours before serving. With a sharp knife, thinly slice the fillet and serve with accompaniments of your choosing.

CRISPY COCONUT SHRIMP LETTUCE CUPS

Serves 2 to 4

Dipping Sauce

½ cup fresh lime juice, plus
more as needed

1 Tbsp lime zest

1 small ruby red grapefruit,
juice with pulp

2 Tbsp fish sauce

1 Tbsp palm, light brown,
or coconut sugar

4 garlic cloves, thinly
sliced lengthwise
on a mandoline

1 shallot, finely minced

1 fresh serrano chile, thinly
sliced into rounds, plus
more as needed

1 fresh Fresno chile, halved,
seeded, and cut into
thin strips, plus more
as needed

1 small carrot, julienned

Shrimp

2 cups coconut, grapeseed,
or canola oil, for frying

2 cups rice flour

1 cup unsweetened
desiccated coconut,
toasted, plus more
for serving

¼ cup tapioca flour

1 tsp kosher salt

2 tsp granulated sugar

1 tsp ground allspice

1 lb large shrimp, peeled
and deveined, with
tails left on

Freshly ground black
pepper

One 12 oz can cold seltzer

Lettuce Cups

8 to 12 large butterhead
or other firm, flexible
lettuce leaves

½ cup mixed fresh herbs,
such as mint, parsley,
cilantro, and dill, for
serving

Crispy shrimp wrapped in refreshing herbs and lettuces? Yes, please! We love the combination of textures that this dish provides. It makes a great lunch platter, and it's also a fun starter for a dinner party. To simplify your day-of prep, make the dipping sauce ahead of time. You want to achieve a tangy sauce with lots of umami, fresh citrus flavor, and a blooming heat from the peppers.

TO MAKE THE DIPPING SAUCE: In a small bowl, combine the lime zest and juice, grapefruit juice, fish sauce, palm sugar, garlic, shallot, serrano chile, Fresno chile, and carrot. Stir to combine and taste. Add more chiles for extra heat, or more lime juice for extra acid. Use immediately or store in an airtight container in the refrigerator for up to 1 week. (It works well with rice, noodles, and salads.)

TO MAKE THE SHRIMP: In a heavy-bottomed pot (like a Dutch oven) over medium-high, heat the coconut oil to 350°F on a thermometer (see frying guidelines, page 45). Line a sheet pan with paper towels and set near the stove.

In a medium bowl, combine the rice flour, toasted coconut, tapioca flour, salt, sugar, and allspice and whisk thoroughly. Taste to ensure a balance of sweet and salty.

Generously season the shrimp with salt and pepper.

Slowly add the cold seltzer (but not the whole can) to the batter to achieve the thickness of pancake batter. Drop 4 to 6 shrimp in the batter, coating them thoroughly, then carefully lower the shrimp into the hot oil and fry, flipping once, until golden brown, 1 to 2 minutes per side. Transfer the shrimp to the paper towels and season with a bit more salt. Fry the remaining shrimp, adjusting the heat as needed to keep the oil at 350°F.

TO SERVE: Arrange lettuce leaves in a corner of a serving platter and a pile of shrimp in another corner. Place a small bowl of dipping sauce on the platter. Garnish the platter with the herbs and a pinch or two of toasted coconut. Have your guests make little wraps for each shrimp with the lettuces and herbs and dip them in the sauce! Enjoy!

Roses Are Red, Violets Are Blue, There Is No Limit to Our Love for Fried Food

When we love something as much as we love fried food, we want it to have a soul mate—we want it to be happy. More specifically, we want fried food's soul mate to be a frizzante rosé. We're not here to tell you how to love or who to love, but we are here to say that it's hard to deny the compatibility of a crispy, golden-brown bite of heaven and a dry, luxuriously sparkling rosé bursting with personality. Frizzante wines, made in Italy, are characterized by a smaller, finer bubble—to us, they are the cashmere of sparkling wines. A good frizzante rosé is the ideal "yes and" wine for any fried-food moment; it will leave you with renewed vigor and zest for the rest of your meal.

CHARRED CABBAGE WITH SAMBAL AND QUESO COTIJA

Serves 4

Sambal

3 Tbsp minced anchovies
2 Tbsp Fragrant Chile Oil
    (page 38)
2 Tbsp fish sauce
6 garlic cloves, minced
Zest and juice of 4 limes
    (about ½ cup juice)
4 scallions, thinly sliced
2 fresh Fresno chiles or
    long peppers, minced
One 1 in knob ginger,
    peeled and minced
1 medium shallot, minced
4 scallions

Cabbage

1 head red cabbage
2 Tbsp extra-virgin olive oil
Kosher salt
¼ cup crumbled
    cotija cheese
¼ cup chopped
    cilantro leaves

There are rumored to be as many as three hundred varieties of sambal in the Indonesian archipelago. To describe it in broad strokes, sambal is a sauce made of chiles, often with ginger, shallot, and tomato, and sometimes with shrimp, sugar, or tamarind. It pairs well with any dish that desires a fresh, spicy, pungent kick, which, if you ask us, is every dish. In this recipe, we drizzle sambal into the smoky sweet crevices of charred cabbage. A generous sprinkle of cotija, an aged Mexican cheese with a salty, earthy funk, provides necessary creaminess to balance the piquant sambal. An unlikely pairing indeed, but aren't those the best? Use leftover sambal to top roasted meat or fish, or to add some heat to a vinaigrette.

TO MAKE THE SAMBAL: In a small bowl, combine the anchovies, chile oil, fish sauce, garlic, lime zest and juice, scallions, chiles, ginger, and shallot. Set aside to allow the flavors to bloom while you make the cabbage. Store leftover sambal in an airtight container in the refrigerator for up to 2 weeks.

TO MAKE THE CABBAGE: Set a rack in the middle of the oven and preheat the oven to 500°F. Line a baking sheet with aluminum foil.

    With a chef's knife, cut the cabbage lengthwise in half through the core then into 8 equal wedges. Arrange the wedges on the prepared baking sheet, drizzle all over with olive oil, and season lightly with salt. Roast in the middle of the oven for 10 minutes then flip the wedges over and roast until the cabbage is tender and has started to brown and char on the top and bottom, about 10 more minutes.

TO SERVE: Place the cabbage wedges on a platter and drizzle generously with sambal. Garnish with cotija and cilantro and enjoy.

There's a New It Girl in Town

Skin-contact white wine, the artist formerly known as "orange wine," has been the It Girl of natural wine for years. If you, like us, find these wines to be a versatile and welcome addition to any meal, consider an oft-overlooked alternative: darker rosés. The levels of acid and tannin in orange wine are often similar to darker rosés, which are sometimes referred to as gem-toned rosés or rosatos. Rosato refers to an Italian style of rosé known for being darker, because the red Italian varietals used have higher tannins and pigments in their skins due to climate and sun exposure. We recommend rosatos in particular with this dish, because their tannins can stand up to the char of the cabbage and the spice of the sambal, but the wine still has enough acid and lightness to cut through the heat of the dish.

SALCHIPAPAS BRAVAS WITH NOT-SO-SECRET SAUCES

Serves 2 to 4

Potatoes
10 to 15 small Yukon
    Gold potatoes
3 lbs kosher salt

Salsa Brava
½ cup mayonnaise
1 Tbsp white distilled
    vinegar
2 tsp ground coriander
1½ tsp achiote paste
1 tsp kosher salt
1 garlic clove, peeled
1 small orange

Mustard Mayo
Sauce
¼ cup whole-grain mustard
1 Tbsp mustard powder
1 tsp ground turmeric
1 tsp kosher salt
1 small orange
¼ cup mayonnaise

Salchicha
8 cups canola oil
3 or 4 hot dogs

For Serving
Chile Dust (page 37)
Kosher salt
1 bunch scallions,
    thinly sliced
Quick Citrus Pickle
    (page 41)
1 fresh Fresno chile,
    thinly sliced

This is our take on a classic street vendor snack from Ecuador and Peru, often enjoyed by children as an after-school snack. Salchipapas consists of French fries and hot dogs deep fried and slathered in sauces, as is our proclivity. Our recipe is a mashup of the street snack and patatas bravas, the ubiquitous Spanish tapa, made with crispy fried potatoes and typically served with brava sauce and garlic mayo. Of course, even the patatas bravas part of this recipe is a spin on tradition, as our sauce is seasoned with orange and achiote paste, and our mayo is flavored with mustard and turmeric. The sauces and spice mix can be made in advance and last several weeks in the fridge. If you are vegetarian, fear not! Proceed as instructed, sans hot dogs. It's just as good!

TO MAKE THE POTATOES: Preheat the oven to 400°F.

In a shallow, rimmed baking dish, cover the potatoes with the salt. Cover the dish with aluminum foil and roast until the potatoes are fork tender, 1 to 1½ hours. Remove from the oven and cool slightly before flipping the pan onto a baking sheet. Let stand until the potatoes are cool but not cold. Smash the potatoes between your hands until they are about ¾ in thick. Set aside.

TO MAKE THE SALSA BRAVA: In a blender, combine the mayonnaise, vinegar, coriander, achiote paste, salt, garlic, and zest and juice of the orange and blend on high until smooth. Use right away to make salchipapas bravas or store in an airtight container in the refrigerator for up to 1 month.

TO MAKE THE MUSTARD MAYO SAUCE: In a blender, combine the mustard, mustard powder, turmeric, salt, and zest and juice of the orange and blend until smooth. Transfer to a bowl, add the mayonnaise, and whisk until fully combined. Taste and add additional salt if needed. Use right away to make salchipapas bravas or store in an airtight container in the refrigerator for up to 1 month.

TO MAKE THE SALCHICHA: Cut the hot dogs crosswise into 2 or 3 in long pieces. Deeply score an X into one end of each piece, so it curls up like an octopus when fried.

In a medium-size heavy-bottomed pot over medium, heat the canola oil to 350°F on a deep-fry/candy thermometer (see frying guidelines, page 45). Line two baking sheets with paper towels and set near the stove or a deep fryer.

When the oil reaches 350°F, carefully add the smashed potatoes and work in batches to avoid overcrowding. Fry, turning with tongs or a slotted spoon, until golden brown, 3 to 5 minutes. Transfer the potatoes to one of

the paper towel–lined baking sheets. Fry the remaining potatoes, adjusting the heat as needed to keep the oil at 350°F.

Keeping the oil at 350°F, carefully add all the hot dog pieces and fry, turning with tongs or a slotted spoon, until puffy and crispy, about 2 minutes. Transfer to the other paper towel–lined baking sheet. Fry the remaining hot dogs, adjusting the heat as needed to keep the oil at 350°F.

TO SERVE: In a large bowl, toss the potatoes and hot dogs with a generous amount of chile dust. Season with salt. Add half of the scallions and toss. Transfer to a serving platter and drizzle with zigzags of salsa brava and mustard mayo. Sprinkle with pickled onions, chiles, and the remaining scallions. Serve immediately to a group of adoring friends, eat with your fingers, and lick them clean.

SPICY CHORIZO LARB

Serves 4 to 6

Rice Powder

¼ cup jasmine rice

Larb

½ cup palm, coconut,
    or light brown sugar

¼ cup fish sauce

1 Tbsp neutral oil

1 lb freshly ground,
    uncured Mexican-
    style chorizo

4 garlic cloves, minced

One 2 in piece ginger,
    peeled and minced

1 lemongrass stalk, minced

1 shallot, minced

1 fresh jalapeño, serrano, or
    Thai chile, thinly sliced

2 cups roughly chopped
    fresh herbs, such
    as mint, cilantro,
    and/or dill

2 Tbsp freshly squeezed
    lime juice, plus 2 limes,
    cut into wedges

Crisp lettuce or cabbage
    wedges, for serving

Fragrant Chile Oil (page
    38), for garnish

Our spin on this classic Thai and Laotian dish makes a perfect summertime snack. Traditionally, larb is a cold dish with ground or chopped meat mixed with toasted rice flour that can be served cooked or raw. We use a Mexican-style chorizo, but feel free to experiment with different proteins, such as leftover fish or chicken from last night's dinner. We serve our larb alongside a bed of crisp lettuces and cabbage for wrapping the meat into little bundles. Bright, rich, and spicy, this dish delights from the inside out.

TO MAKE THE RICE POWDER: Preheat the oven to 350°F.

Spread the rice evenly on a baking sheet and toast until aromatic and golden brown, 6 to 8 minutes. Transfer to a blender or spice grinder and blend into a medium-fine powder. Set aside.

TO MAKE THE LARB: In a small saucepan over medium heat, slowly melt the sugar until it turns a deep golden brown. Immediately remove from the heat and gradually add the fish sauce, stirring constantly with a wooden spoon. If the fish sauce caramel stiffens, briefly return it to low heat, stirring, until loosened. Set aside.

In a large frying pan over high heat, warm the neutral oil. Remove the chorizo from its casing and break it down with your hands. Add the chorizo to the pan and cook, breaking up any chunks with a wooden spoon, until browned, about 6 minutes. Lower the heat to a simmer then add the garlic, ginger, and lemongrass and cook, stirring, for another 3 to 4 minutes. Remove from the heat and then add the fish sauce caramel and stir well to incorporate. Transfer the mixture to a medium bowl and let cool slightly.

Once the chorizo has cooled, break up any clumps and mix in the fat that may have set—it's part of the deep umami pleasure of this dish. Add the shallot, chile, and a fistful of herbs and gently toss to combine. Season with the lime juice, sprinkle with 1 to 2 Tbsp of rice powder, and toss again. Season as needed—your mouth experience should be dynamic, with the fattiness of the meat surrounded by bright acid from the lime juice and crunch from the herbs and rice powder.

TO SERVE: Arrange a scoop of larb on a serving platter and sprinkle with rice powder and herbs. Add lime wedges to the platter. A drizzle of Fragrant Chile Oil never hurts. On a separate plate, place lettuce and/or cabbage, separating their leaves and arranging them beautifully and bountifully. Eat using your vehicle of choice, be it a lettuce or cabbage cup, adding a scoop of chorizo and a pinch of herbs to each bite. No forks, no spoons, no problem.

PATACON PISAO

Serves 3 to 4

Pork Belly

1 lb pork belly

1 Tbsp kosher salt

1 cup freshly squeezed
orange juice

1 cup apple cider vinegar

3 Tbsp soy sauce

2 Tbsp whole-grain mustard

1 Tbsp granulated sugar

5 garlic gloves, smashed
and peeled

2 fresh chiles de árbol

1 cup frying flour mix
(see page 46; or
all-purpose flour)

Kosher salt

Plantains

3 or 4 unripe green
plantains (1 per person)

2 qts canola oil

Kosher salt

For Serving

One 12 oz can refried
beans

3 Tbsp crumbled cotija
cheese

3 Tbsp Quick Citrus Pickle
(page 41)

2 Tbsp chopped cilantro

2 Tbsp Pickled Mustard
Seeds (page 44)

In Spanish, "pisao" is derived from the word "pisado" and translates to "stepped on." Popular across Colombia, Ecuador, and Venezuela, the green plantain is smashed thin and smothered in toppings that differ from region to region. Our recipe requires several steps, so we recommend completing it over two days. Green plantains will temporarily stain your hands, but it's OK—you're a sexy, dirty, glamorous chef with connection to your sustenance! Often served as a plantain sandwich, our version is open-faced. To put extra pep in your step, listen to this recipe's namesake song, "Patacon Pisao" by Johnny Ventura, as you work :)

One Day Ahead

TO MAKE THE PORK BELLY: Preheat the oven to 325°F. Season the pork belly on both sides with the kosher salt. In a Dutch oven, combine the orange juice, vinegar, soy sauce, mustard, sugar, garlic, chiles, and 1 cup of water. Nestle the pork belly, skin side up, in the braising liquid. Cover with the lid and bake until tender, about 2 hours. Remove the pork belly from the braising liquid and let cool at room temperature. Pour the braising liquid through a fine-mesh sieve into a bowl; discard any solids. Cover the strained braising liquid and refrigerate overnight.

Once the pork belly has reached room temperature, wrap it in plastic and put it on a baking sheet. Put a second baking sheet on top of the pork belly then put cans or a heavy pan on top to gently weigh down the pork. Refrigerate overnight.

The Next Day

Use a spoon to scoop out and discard the fat that has solidified at the top of the braising liquid. In a small pot over low heat, bring the braising liquid to a boil then turn the heat to low and simmer until it begins to thicken and become syrupy, about 20 minutes. Turn off the heat and let cool.

While the liquid is reducing, pull out your pressed pork belly, cut it lengthwise into 2 in wide sections and then cut each section across the grain into ½ in thick pieces. Set aside.

TO MAKE THE PLANTAINS: Cut off the ends off the plantains and slide your thumb or fingers under the skin to peel them.

In a large heavy-bottomed pot over medium heat, heat the canola oil to 350°F on a deep-fry/candy thermometer (see frying guidelines, page 45). Line two baking sheets with paper towels and set near the stove or a deep fryer.

When the oil reaches 350°F, carefully add 1 plantain and fry, turning with tongs or a slotted spoon, until golden brown, about 5 minutes. Transfer

to one of the paper towel–lined baking sheets then use a large plate to smash the hot plantains into flattish half moons. Fry the remaining plantains, adjusting the heat as needed to keep the oil at 350°F. After frying and smashing all the plantains, fry each plantain again, turning with tongs or a slotted spoon, until crispy and golden, about 2 minutes. Return to the paper towel–lined baking sheet and season generously with salt on both sides.

Make sure the oil is still at 350°F. Put the frying flour mix in a bowl.

Working in batches, dredge the pork belly pieces in the frying flour mix then carefully add to the hot oil and fry, turning with tongs or a slotted spoon, until crisp and golden, 5 to 6 minutes. Transfer to the other paper towel–lined baking sheet and season with salt. Fry the remaining pork belly, adjusting the heat as needed to keep the oil at 350°F.

TO SERVE: In a small pot over low heat, warm the refried beans. Slather a thick layer of beans on each fried plantain and top with pieces of fried pork belly. Arrange on a serving platter and sprinkle with cotija, pickled onion, cilantro, and pickled mustard seeds. Drizzle with the reduced braising liquid and serve immediately.

"KIBBICHE" PARTY PLATTER

Serves a party! (About 24 pieces)

Total cook time about 3 hours

Onion Relish

3 Tbsp white distilled vinegar
1 Tbsp harissa
2 tsp Fragrant Chile Oil (page 38)
2 tsp kosher salt
1 white onion, minced

Cumin-Citrus Yogurt

1 cup full-fat Greek yogurt
1 tsp ground cumin
1 tsp kosher salt
Zest and juice of 1 orange
Zest and juice of 1 lime
6 sprigs cilantro, chopped

Filling

1 Tbsp extra-virgin olive oil
6 garlic cloves, minced
1 shallot or small onion, minced
1 lb ground beef
1 Tbsp smoked paprika
1 Tbsp sumac
1 Tbsp kosher salt
2 tsp ground cumin
1 tsp freshly ground black pepper
¼ cup chopped parsley leaves
¼ cup chopped cilantro leaves and stems
3 Tbsp pine nuts, toasted and finely chopped
2 qt neutral oil, for frying

This dish is a happy marriage between Ecuadorian corviche and Middle Eastern kibbeh. Both are stuffed, football-shaped patties. From the Ecuadorian coast, corviche is made with green plantain and is usually stuffed with tuna or salted cod, called bacalao. Kibbeh, usually formed with bulgar wheat and ground beef or lamb, is found in the food cultures of Mexico, Columbia, and Brazil, due to the transmigration of Levantine communities to South and Central America in the early twentieth century. Feel free to make the relish and yogurt sauce ahead of time. The kibbiches can also be formed a day ahead (or frozen up to three months) to make your party prep more manageable, and we encourage inviting a friend to assist you in the process!

TO MAKE THE ONION RELISH: In a bowl, combine the vinegar, harissa, chile oil, and salt. Add half of the onion and stir to coat; reserve the remaining onion for the casing. Let the relish marinate for at least 30 minutes before serving. Store the onion relish in an airtight container in the refrigerator for up to 1 week.

TO MAKE THE CUMIN-CITRUS YOGURT: In a small bowl, combine the yogurt, cumin, salt, orange zest and juice, lime zest and juice, and the cilantro. Whisk to combine. Adjust the salt and acid levels as needed. Transfer to an airtight container and refrigerate until ready to use or for up to 1 week.

TO MAKE THE FILLING: In a cast-iron skillet over low heat, warm the olive oil. Add the garlic and onion and cook, stirring, until soft and translucent, 5 to 7 minutes. Add the beef, paprika, sumac, salt, cumin, and pepper and stir to combine. Turn the heat to medium and cook, stirring, until the meat is browned and cooked through, about 5 minutes. Turn off the heat and let cool slightly then add the parsley, cilantro, and pine nuts. Adjust the seasoning as needed and let cool to room temperature.

TO MAKE THE KIBBICHE: Cut off the ends off the plantains and slide your thumb or fingers under the skin to peel them. Cut 4 of the plantains into 1 in pieces, put in a medium pot, and cover with water. Add the garlic, season with salt, and bring to a boil. Turn down the heat to medium and simmer until fork-tender, 15 to 20 minutes. Transfer the plantains to a food processor and, add the tahini, cumin, and the onion reserved from the relish. Pulse until a smooth dough forms, then transfer to a large bowl.

Using the grater attachment for the food processor or the medium-grain side of a box grater, grate the remaining 4 plantains. Add to the cooked plantain mixture and knead to create a uniform dough.

Kibbiche

8 unripe green plantains

10 garlic cloves, peeled
    and halved lengthwise

Kosher salt

3 Tbsp tahini paste

2 Tbsp ground cumin

For Serving

1 Tbsp Aleppo pepper

2 Tbsp chopped cilantro

Start making the kibbiche immediately, or refrigerate until ready. Fill a small bowl with cool water to help keep the dough from sticking to your fingers. Line a baking sheet with parchment paper. Divide the dough into 24 equal balls (about ⅓ cup each). Dip your fingers into the water and use them to flatten each ball into a pancake shape. Put about a tablespoon of filling in the center of each pancake then fold one side of the pancake over to form a semicircle. Gently pinch closed the edges of the semicircle to seal the dough. Dipping your fingers in the water as needed, push the dough into itself, cupping the kibbiche between the Ls of your thumb and forefinger to create a football-shaped croquette. Repeat to make more kibbiche and arrange on the parchment-lined baking sheet. Fry right away or refrigerate overnight. Kibbiches can also be well wrapped and frozen for up to 3 months.

In a large heavy-bottomed pot over medium-high, heat the neutral oil to 350°F on a deep-fry thermometer (see frying guidelines, page 45). Line a baking sheet with paper towels and set near the stove or a deep fryer.

When the oil reaches 350°F, carefully add 4 or 5 croquettes and fry, turning with tongs or a slotted spoon, until hot on the inside and a deep golden brown color on the outside, 4 to 6 minutes. Transfer the croquettes to the paper towel–lined baking sheet. Continue to fry, adjusting the heat as needed to keep the oil at 350°F.

TO SERVE: Gently score each kibbiche lengthwise so the filling peeks out (yonic vibes). Add a dollop of cumin-citrus yogurt to the center, followed by a spoonful of onion relish, and finish with a sprinkle of Aleppo pepper and cilantro. Arrange on a large platter. Voila!

Soup

In the wintertime, a hot broth can warm you to your bones, and be the ultimate nourishment, but please also consider the merits of a steamy, spicy soup on a hot summer's day. It can be just the thing you need to cure a cold, a hangover, or a bad mood, as you simultaneously sweat out all the toxins and rehydrate your system. Who doesn't need that?

Soups are versatile; they can be a humble workhorse or the star of the show. They can be served all year-round, as a simple meal on their own (Sopa de Pan, page 151), or as the centerpiece of a festive dinner party (Seafood Moqueca, page 203). We always have at least one soup on our menu, the Caldito de Pollo (page 158), and often a rotating list of other seasonal recipes. There are a few regulars who come in weekly on a date with themselves and order a caldito. The "solo caldito" is one that makes us want to pause on cooking everything else, even when we are deep in the weeds on a busy night and take some time to put in a little extra love.

SOPA DE PAN

Serves 2

2 Tbsp unsalted butter
1 Tbsp annatto seeds
1 bunch scallions,
    finely chopped
2 cups whole milk
Leaves from 3 sprigs
    of oregano
Kosher salt to taste
1 tsp freshly ground
    black pepper
½ cup crumbled
    queso fresco
1 day-old baguette, cut
    into 1 in thick slices
Cilantro, for garnish
Fragrant Chile Oil
    (page 38)

This simple recipe is a nod to the fundamentals of nourishment and necessity: When we have little, we make do with what we have, to ensure the bellies of those we love are full. Stale bread can make a simple broth more filling and, in fact, if you look into the etymology of the word "soup," it originally meant "bread soaked in broth." Our bread soup is a translation of an Ecuadorian recipe that sometimes calls for meat-based stock, but our version calls for the humble mixture of milk and water. Make it when you need a warm hug or don't feel like making a trip to the grocery store.

In a medium pot over medium heat, warm the butter. Add the annatto seeds and toast until the butter turns red-orange in color. Remove the seeds from the pan and discard. Set aside a small handful of the scallions for garnish then add the rest to the pot and sauté until wilted, about 1 minute. Add the milk, oregano, salt, pepper, and 1 cup of water and bring to a simmer. Add the queso fresco, cover, and simmer on low for 5 minutes. Be careful not to boil the soup. Add the slices of day-old bread, stirring so they soak up the broth.

TO SERVE: Divide among bowls, sprinkle with the cilantro and reserved scallions, and add a dash of chile oil.

BORSCHT CON BOLAS

Serves 4 (10 to 12 dumplings)

Borscht

4 Tbsp butter

1 cup diced celery

1 medium yellow
    onion, diced

1 leek, diced

Kosher salt

Freshly ground
    black pepper

5 garlic cloves, minced

3 Tbsp minced ginger

1 tsp ground turmeric

4 medium golden
    beets, grated

2 carrots, peeled and
    cut into ½ in rounds

2 medium potatoes,
    peeled and cut into
    1 in dice

8 cups water or your
    stock of choice

Dumplings

2 unripe green plantains

2 Tbsp plus 1 tsp
    kosher salt

2 garlic cloves, minced

1 large egg

2 Tbsp chopped dill

¼ tsp ground turmeric

1 Tbsp apple cider
    vinegar

½ lemon

Sour cream and
    chopped dill,
    for garnish

A love child born from two regionally unique soups separated by oceans and continents, this recipe blends Eastern European borscht with coastal Ecuadoran sopa de bolas de verde. Both soups symbolize comfort to the people who know them, and traditionally call for meat and bone broth, but we have opted for a perfectly satisfying vegetarian version! The green plantain bola dumplings, which can be made a day in advance, add body and depth of flavor to the sweet and sour borscht broth.

TO MAKE THE BORSCHT: In a heavy-bottomed stockpot or Dutch oven, melt 2 Tbsp of the butter. Add the celery, onion, and leek, season with salt and pepper, and sauté until soft and translucent, about 6 minutes. Stir in the garlic, ginger, and turmeric and sauté for 1 minute. Add the beets, carrots, and potatoes, along with the water or stock, and bring to a boil. Turn the heat to low and simmer until the vegetables are soft and fork-tender, 25 to 30 minutes. Season with salt.

TO MAKE THE DUMPLINGS: Peel the green plantains by slicing off the ends and running a knife along them lengthwise; slide your thumb in between the skin and the flesh and peel the skin.

Fill a medium pot with water, add 2 Tbsp of the salt, and bring to a boil. Cut one of the plantains crosswise into four pieces and add to the boiling water. Turn the heat to low and simmer until fork-tender, about 20 minutes. Remove the plantain and cool slightly, but don't allow to cool completely, as it will dry out and toughen up, making it harder to form into dumplings. In a food processor, pulse the boiled plantain into a sticky dough with a few lumps. Transfer to a medium bowl.

With the grater attachment of the food processor or the medium-grain side of a box grater, grate the remaining raw plantain then add it to the cooked plantain. Add the garlic, egg, dill, turmeric, and the remaining 1 tsp of salt and mix with one hand until thoroughly combined. With a firm touch, form the plantain mash into 10 to 12 balls, each one slightly smaller than a golf ball. Set aside.

TO SERVE: Gingerly drop the dumplings into the hot simmering broth and add the apple cider vinegar. Cook, without stirring, over low heat until the dumplings are plump, 10 to 15 minutes. Using a slotted spoon, divide the dumplings among soup bowls. Quickly add the remaining 2 Tbsp of butter to the soup and stir to incorporate. Ladle the broth and vegetables into each bowl. Spritz each bowl with the ½ lemon. Garnish with a healthy dollop of sour cream and plenty of chopped dill.

BROWN RICE CONGEE

Serves 2 to 4

2 cups dried mushrooms,
   such as shiitake, porcini,
   or black trumpet
½ sheet kombu
½ cup short grain
   brown rice
2 Tbsp pearl barley
1 Tbsp minced ginger
1 Tbsp soy sauce
1 Tbsp umeboshi vinegar
1 tsp mushroom powder
2 tsp toasted sesame oil
1 tsp kosher salt
⅛ tsp freshly ground
   white pepper
2 to 4 large eggs
Tender greens, such as
   pea shoots or tatsoi
   (optional)
3 scallions, sliced
½ cup chopped roasted
   peanuts
1 Tbsp white sesame seeds
Cilantro sprigs, for garnish

There are as many names for rice porridge as there are variations and styles. Spanning across Asia, as well as Portugal and Brazil, you can find congee, juk, lugaw, kanji, or canja, all cooked with a wide variety of flavors and accoutrements. No matter where you live, rice cooked for a prolonged period is a stick-to-your-bones meal that is often given to postpartum mothers, people recovering from sickness, or as a baby's first food. Our version is vegetarian, and it's perfect for breakfast or as a simple but deeply nourishing dinner. We use brown rice for its nutritional value, but you could substitute white rice, just keep in mind that it will shorten the cooking time a bit, so defer to your instincts.

In a stockpot, combine the dried mushrooms, kombu, and 8 cups of water and bring to a boil. Turn off the heat and steep until the mushrooms have softened and their flavor has permeated the water, 20 to 30 minutes.

Pour the mushroom stock through a fine-mesh sieve into another stockpot; reserve the mushrooms. Add the brown rice, barley, and ginger and bring to a boil. Turn the heat to low and gently simmer, stirring frequently to avoid burning, for about 1 hour. As it simmers, the mushroom stock will thicken and be absorbed into the rice and barley. If you prefer a looser porridge, gradually add water, ½ cup at a time. Once the rice is broken down and the texture is like a loose oatmeal, stir in the soy sauce, fish sauce, sesame oil, salt, and white pepper.

When the porridge is in its last few minutes of cooking, in a small pot of water, cook the eggs for 8 minutes. Remove from the heat and quickly cool under very cold running water to stop the cooking process. Set aside.

Cut the reserved mushrooms crosswise into thin slivers for garnish.

TO SERVE: Stir the tender greens, if using, and half of the scallions into the congee and divide among bowls. Garnish with the sliced mushrooms, peanuts, sesame seeds, cilantro sprigs, and the remaining scallions. Peel the eggs, cut each one in half, and then nestle a half into each bowl. Exhale, take a bite, and experience the comfort.

HAM BONE AND HOMINY PORRIDGE

Serves 4 to 6

1 lb cracked hominy

1 lb smoked ham hock

6 garlic cloves, smashed and peeled

1 to 2 Tbsp kosher salt

1 tsp smoked paprika, plus more for serving

½ tsp ground turmeric

2 Tbsp unsalted butter

½ red onion, thinly sliced into half moons, for serving

Hominy is an Indigenous American food found across the Americas and the Caribbean, and it is used as a base for drinks, soups, stews, and other dishes. The whole kernels are the star ingredient in the Mexican stew pozole, but they can also be finely ground to make masa, which is integral to Latin American cuisine, especially for making tortillas, arepas, tamales, and pupusas. In Jamaica, cracked hominy is cooked with cinnamon and coconut milk for a classic breakfast; our dish draws from this in form but with more savory character. We love hominy for its subtle earthy corn flavor, which creates comforting nostalgia when topped with butter. This recipe is similar, in terms of bone-sticking comfort, to our brown rice congee, but with a flavor profile more reminiscent of grits, resulting in a taste that evokes the North American South. Don't forget to soak your hominy one day ahead.

One Day Ahead

In a medium-size stockpot, cover the hominy with at least 4 inches of cold water and soak overnight.

The Next Day

When ready to cook, strain the hominy. In a large heavy-bottomed stockpot or Dutch oven, combine the hominy, ham hock, and garlic. Cover with water (about 12 cups) and bring to a boil. Turn the heat to medium, cover slightly ajar, and simmer gently, stirring occasionally to avoid burning. Add water if the level drops below the hominy, until the hominy kernels soften and release their starch, fat melts off the ham hock, and the meat is meltingly tender, about 3 hours. Bite into a kernel to make sure it's ready—it should fall apart easily and be fairly moist inside. Most of the liquid should be absorbed, and the porridge should be thick and creamy.

Remove the ham hock and set aside to cool. Season the hominy with salt, add the paprika and turmeric, and cook for 10 more minutes. When cool enough to handle, pick the meat off the ham hock, discarding any bones. Coarsely chop the larger pieces of meat and any gelatinous bits of skin (it's really fatty and melts right in) and return to the hominy. Add a splash of water if the hominy seems too thick. Add the butter and stir until well incorporated. Serve in bowls and garnish with a dash of paprika and sliced raw onion.

CALDITO DE POLLO

Serves 2 to 4

Soup

1 whole chicken,
   3 to 5 lbs
3 carrots, peeled and
   halved crosswise
3 small Yukon Gold
   potatoes, peeled
2 small onions, peeled
   and halved
2 celery stalks, halved
Kosher salt
2 Tbsp unsalted butter
   (optional)

Garnishes

Avocado halves, lime
   wedges, diced red
   onion, minced cilantro,
   chopped scallion,
   chopped dill

Optional Additions

Corn on the cob, sweet
   potatoes, rutabaga,
   grated ginger, minced
   jalapeño, rice or oats
   dropped into the soup
   while it's cooking, an
   egg or two

Comforting and nourishing, chicken soup is an integral part of food cultures worldwide. Our interpretation is inspired by versions found in food stalls throughout Central and South America. This recipe functions like a happy memory of childhood, soft and fuzzy and warm. The addition of butter at the end is not traditional and can be omitted, but it adds a touch so comforting and surprisingly special, we're sure you won't regret it. We garnish with avocados, limes, red onions, cilantro, scallions, and dill.

In a stockpot over medium heat, cover the chicken with 5 qts of water and bring to a boil. Using a ladle, skim any foam and transfer it to a bowl. (See stock guidelines, page 46.) Add the carrots, potatoes, onion, and celery. Turn the heat to low and gently simmer, skimming any foam from the surface every 20 minutes, until the stock is golden in color and tastes like chicken, at least 1½ hours.

Meanwhile, lovingly prepare your garnish tray. Mince the herbs and other garnishes of your choice. We like to combine the herbs into a vibrant herb mix. The broth you are preparing is your blank canvas, the garnishes are your paints. Express yourself!

When the stock has simmered for at least 1½ hours, taste it. If it doesn't quite taste chicken-y enough, cook it for a little longer, but not more than 3 hours. The chicken should begin to fall off the bone, and the stock should be deeply flavored. Carefully remove the chicken and vegetables from the stock and place on a tray or in a bowl; keep warm for serving. Pour the stock through a fine-mesh sieve and return it to the pot. Put over low heat and season with enough salt (at least 2 tsp) to deepen the flavors, so the stock tastes more like itself, with a sweet background of softly singing vegetables. Stir in the butter, if using. If you're adding the corn, drop it in the hot broth right before serving to quickly blanch.

TO SERVE: Divide the reserved cooked veggies among big soup bowls. When the chicken is cool enough to touch (but still hot), break it down to your liking. We like to serve the soup with a whole drumstick or a big piece of breast, but you can also pick the meat off the bone before serving if preferred. Finally, ladle the hot broth over the chicken and vegetables, and let everyone garnish their own portions with avocado, lime, red onion, cilantro, scallion, and/or dill.

Drink What Feels Good

The caldito de pollo is a chameleon in the world of pairings: a robust red, a cheeky orange, a rosé with something to say, or an elegant white—they all work! It is easy to get swept up in institutional systems that fixate on whether a pairing is right or wrong. Remember that both food and wine are sources of comfort and replenishment, so take it easy on yourself when thinking about what wine to choose for dinner.

CHORIZO Y FIDEOS

Serves 4 to 6

Shrimp Butter

1 cup (2 sticks) unsalted
    butter
Shells from 1 lb of shrimp

Fideos

4 Tbsp neutral oil
One 8 oz package fideos
    or angel hair pasta,
    broken into 2 to 3 in
    pieces
½ lb freshly ground,
    uncured Mexican-
    style chorizo
1½ tsp cumin seeds
½ medium onion, diced
5 garlic cloves, minced
½ tsp cayenne pepper
1 medium carrot, peeled
    and diced
One 15 oz can crushed
    tomatoes
One 15 oz can garbanzo
    beans (do not drain;
    or 2 cups cooked
    garbanzos)
¼ cup fish sauce
Kosher salt
Cilantro sprigs, lime
    wedges, and Fragrant
    Chile Oil (page 38),
    for garnish

Somewhere between a soup and a stew, this dish reminds us of an elegant, grownup version of SpaghettiOs but made with Mexican-style chorizo and a short vermicelli-like noodle. You could swap out the shrimp butter for regular unsalted butter, but we will feel sorry that you won't know the insane flavor party you are missing. You can also use the shrimp butter to season popcorn or add richness and depth to any seafood dish.

One Day Ahead

TO MAKE THE SHRIMP BUTTER: In a medium saucepan over low heat, melt the butter. Add the shrimp shells and stir until toasty and golden in color and richly fragrant (everyone around you will ask, "What is that amazing smell?"), about 10 minutes. Transfer the shells and butter to a blender and blend on high to break up shells and create a homogenous paste. Cover and refrigerate overnight to allow the umami-rich shrimp flavor to permeate the butter.

The Next Day

In a small saucepan over medium-low, remelt the shrimp butter and then push it through a fine-mesh sieve, discarding the pulp. Use right away to make chorizo y fideos or store in an airtight container in the refrigerator for up to 1 month or in the freezer for up to 1 year.

TO MAKE THE FIDEOS: In a large frying pan over medium-high heat, warm 2 Tbsp of the oil. Add the fideos and toast, stirring, until golden brown, about 4 minutes. With a slotted spoon, transfer the fideos to a medium bowl and set aside.

In a medium stockpot over medium-high heat, warm the remaining 2 Tbsp of oil. Remove the chorizo from its casing and crumble it with your hands. Add the chorizo to the pot and cook, breaking up any chunks with a wooden spoon, until it's browned and cooked through, about 5 minutes. With a slotted spoon, transfer the chorizo to the same bowl with the fideos and set aside. Do not clean the stockpot.

Add 2 Tbsp of the shrimp butter, along with the cumin seeds, to the stockpot and toast over medium heat, stirring, until fragrant, about 3 minutes. Add the onion, garlic, and cayenne pepper then turn the heat to low and cook, stirring, until translucent, about 4 minutes. Add the carrot and cook, stirring, until slightly soft, 3 to 5 minutes. Add the tomatoes, garbanzo beans and their liquid, and 3 cups of water and bring to a boil. Turn the heat to low and simmer for 10 minutes. Add the chorizo and fideos, along with the fish sauce, and lightly season with salt (a little fish sauce goes a long way). Turn the heat to medium and simmer until the fideos are soft, about 8 minutes.

TO SERVE: Divide the soup among bowls and garnish with cilantro sprigs, juicy lime wedges, and a swirl of chile oil.

INTERMISSION
Simple Pleasures

The recipes in this chapter are very simple, but don't be fooled: simple doesn't mean boring or plain, and it often requires a lot of patience. Like any strong relationship, we learn to value the quiet moments of togetherness—being at home reading our own books or walking in comfortable silence. These moments teach us that we don't need to fill up space to be interesting to one another or engaged in activity to have fun. Our Intermission recipes teach us to honor moments of stillness for the ways they add peace and harmony to our experience of being passionately alive.

ABUELA'S AROMATIC RICE

Serves 4 to 6

2 Tbsp coconut oil
1 small onion, diced
4 garlic cloves, minced
1½ Tbsp salt
2 cups basmati or
   jasmine rice

Rice is a staple dish in households across the world—a comfort food and daily sustenance. Our recipe honors the way that Carla's grandmother Inés taught her to cook rice as a little girl: with garlic and onion and enough salt to taste the ocean. It's barely a recipe, and more of a twist on a standard process. Little did you know that sautéed garlic and onion could change the game for your everyday rice. It will have everyone asking, "Just what *are* you cooking over there!?" "Just some rice," you'll respond, with a quiet smile.

In a medium pot over medium-high heat, warm the coconut oil. Add the onion and garlic and sauté until translucent and fragrant, about 4 minutes. Add 3 cups of water and the salt and bring to a boil over high heat. Add the rice, turn the heat to medium, and cook, watching carefully, until the rice absorbs enough water that the water level is even with the rice, about 10 minutes. Cover, turn the heat as low as possible, and cook until the water is fully absorbed, about 15 minutes. Fluff with a fork and serve immediately.

Why Cook with Wine?

People across the world have been cooking with wine for centuries. You can braise, deglaze, simmer, marinate, and poach with it. When we cook and drink wine at the same time, the rules of society, gravity, and proper attire go out the window. There are, however, some important things to remember when cooking with wine: Always use a wine you would want to drink, because if you're putting it in your food, you will be tasting it. If a recipe calls for red wine, stick to something medium or lighter bodied, like a Grenache—a red wine that is too tannic, for example, will make your beautiful beans bitter. If a recipe calls for white wine, pick something on the lighter, zestier side—recipes are looking for acid :)

ABUELA'S BLACK BEANS

Serves 4 to 6

1 green bell pepper
1 medium yellow onion,
    peeled and quartered
1 lb dry black turtle
    beans, soaked in
    water overnight
1 cup red wine
1 cup extra-virgin olive oil
Kosher salt to taste
2 Tbsp red wine vinegar

Carla's grandmother Inés, who came to the United States from Ecuador when she was in her twenties, taught herself French gastronomy to become a private chef for some of New York's wealthiest families. She learned to cook to support her young family, and out of this was born a true love and passion for food. Inés has taught us some of her best recipes and is excited for us to share them with you. Carla grew up watching her grandmother at the stove, stirring a big pot of black beans for hours, the most delicious smells emanating from the kitchen. One of those smells is the scent of green peppers roasting. The skin chars and wrinkles as it releases a sweet and smoky aroma into the room. This recipe is a family secret, revealed for you now because everyone deserves to bathe in the joy of Abuela's Black Beans. It's a direct line to bean heaven.

In a cast-iron skillet over very high heat, char the green bell pepper, turning as needed, until its skin is black and blistered. Transfer to a bowl and let cool. Char the onion quarters, turning as needed, until black and blistered on each cut side, then put in the bowl with the pepper. (Alternatively, on a foil-lined baking sheet, broil the pepper and onion quarters, turning halfway through, until black and blistered, about 6 minutes.) Remove the stem from the pepper but leave the skin. Remove the seeds if desired, but they will disappear into the beans, so it doesn't really matter. Set aside.

Strain and rinse the beans. In a Dutch oven over medium-high heat, cover the beans with 8 cups of water and bring to a boil, continuously skimming any foam from the surface to eliminate any bitter flavor from the beans. Turn the heat to medium-low and then add the pepper and onion to the pot and stir. Simmer the beans, stirring occasionally and adding water as needed to keep about ¼ in of liquid above the beans, until they are fully cooked, about 1½ hours. Add the wine, followed by the olive oil, and stir well to combine. Continue simmering, stirring occasionally, until the beans have fully absorbed the liquid—look for a velvety texture that wraps itself around your beans like a little black dress—about 30 minutes. This extra half hour of cooking allows the alcohol in the wine to evaporate, the beans to continue releasing their starchiness, and the olive oil to meld with the rest of the liquid, producing a sauce that has some sheen and a nice, thick body. Add the salt, stir, and simmer for 10 more minutes. Stir in the vinegar.

Now it's time for a taste test. These beans should be smoky, with a bright pop of acid. If they are too sweet, add a dash of salt. If they are too acidic, add a dash of olive oil and cook for 5 more minutes. Remove from the heat and serve immediately or let cool completely and store in an airtight container in the refrigerator for up to 5 days or in the freezer for up to 3 months.

Pro tip:
Salting beans only after they have softened is a myth that we subscribe to.

SPICED LENTILS

Serves 4

¼ cup extra-virgin olive oil
2 Tbsp cumin seeds
2 Tbsp coriander seeds
2 Tbsp black or yellow
    mustard seeds
10 garlic cloves, minced
1 medium onion, diced
1 Tbsp ground turmeric
2 cups dried red lentils
1 Tbsp kosher salt

These spiced lentils deliver flavor and nourishment all in one and recall both the menestras of Ecuador and the dahls of India. Combine them with aromatic rice, pickled red onions, and a side of garlicky greens for the perfect no-meat and three.

In a Dutch oven over low heat, warm the olive oil. Add the cumin, coriander, and mustard seeds and toast until fragrant and beginning to pop, 2 to 3 minutes. Add the garlic and onion and sauté until translucent, about 5 minutes. In a medium bowl, whisk the turmeric into 6 cups of water then add to the pot, along with the lentils. Turn the heat to medium and bring to a boil, stirring frequently to keep the lentils from sticking to the bottom of the pot. Turn the heat to low and simmer until the lentils have cooked through and broken down, 20 to 25 minutes. Season with salt and serve hot or let cool completely and store in an airtight container in the refrigerator for up to 1 week or the freezer for up to 3 months.

GARLICKY COLLARD GREENS

**Serves 1
generously or 2
moderately**

1 bunch collard greens
1 Tbsp olive or canola oil
4 garlic cloves, minced
Kosher salt
1 Tbsp freshly squeezed
    lime juice

Growing up in Alabama, Hannah has a particular fondness for collard greens. Her dad is famous for his collards, cooked low and slow, with bacon and pork bones, over many hours until the hearty greens are meltingly tender. She was excited to learn about a more efficient and fresh cooking technique in the popular Brazilian dish, couve a mineira, which is the inspiration behind our recipe. The greens are quick and easy to prepare and maintain their gorgeous bright green color, and the copious amount of garlic is very much our style. To make it, the only requirements are a sharp knife and the willingness to learn to chiffonade.

To chiffonade the collard greens: On a cutting board, cut along the stem of each leaf, removing all the stems. Divide the leaves into two piles. Stack the leaves from one pile and roll them up tightly. Cut from the outside edge of the roll toward the center, moving your knife in ⅛ in increments to create very fine strips. How thinly you slice will impact how quickly the greens will cook, so take your time. Repeat with the second pile of leaves.

In a large pan over high heat, heat the oil until flaming hot. Add the collard greens and immediately toss. Add the garlic and quickly stir to fully incorporate. Add the lime juice, season generously with salt—we suggest using two 3-finger pinches—and sauté again. The entire cooking process should take 3 to 4 minutes. Serve immediately.

What Is a Wine Poem?

Now that you've got your pots simmering, we invite you to crack open a bottle of the good stuff, sit down with your favorite people, unlock the doors of your mind palace, and make a wine poem.

Wine poems originated during our first summer, late one night after a busy service. We had just gotten our wine and beer license, but we were still learning how to talk about wine. That night we sat around tasting the wine, closing our eyes, swishing it in our mouths, and saying the first thought or feeling that came to mind. Words like "dirty sock" and "first kiss." Soon we were shouting out word associations with every sip. We made a list on a scrap of paper, and the next time we printed our wine menu, we realized we had found something special. The exercise felt like an articulation of something essential, a new manifestation of our commitment to accessibility, adventure, and having fun. Why not translate the experience of wine into a language of references that can be understood by most people?

As our library of wine poems grew, so too did our love of making them. No matter how hectic our day was, it became a way to honor and welcome new wines into our oasis. Making time to make the wine poems became a sacred ritual for us. When reviewing wine poems past for this book, each wine came back in a flood of memories. We remember those wines in a way we might have forgotten if not for the wine poems. We wanted to include a "recipe" for a wine poem because even though the concept was developed to help customers figure out what wine to order, the practice of making a wine poem shouldn't be ours to hoard. When you make a poem for a wine, you really get to know it, and the people around you. It's a nonintimidating way to undress a wine and see it in its naked truth. It's a game for everyone to play, and win ;)

Recipe for a Wine Poem

Open a bottle of wine with at least one other person; you cannot make a wine poem alone. Grab paper and a writing utensil, take a sip, close your eyes, and start free associating: Where does the wine go? Where does it take you? What memories does it stir up? Our wine poem word bank will help you get started.

Wine Poem Word Bank ✳ ✳ ✳ slap and tickle, tasseled ottoman, *Heathers*, honeymoon suite, ultrasound, Canal Street, fruits, grass through your blanket, inflatable chair, tusk, wax lips, Shirley Temple, MILF, jelly shoes, baby's breath, negligee, primordial, silt, Feeling Good, moth hair, day off, fontanel, *Overboard*, ponytail, chemtrail, Issey Miyake, taffeta, outie belly button, Patty Hearst, eggshell, static cling, sprinkler, chandelier, purple iris, excavation, leather fetish, burdock, downstream, Silly String, frozen lemonade, chain mail, Tinkerbell, loofah, gel pen, palomino, chrysalis, milk bath, tall grass, Nilla Wafer, whiteboard, bell sleeve, lily crease, figure skate, finishing school, balsa wood, storm's-a-comin', glowworms, survival skills, algae bloom, sweat drip, Flora-Bama, electrolytes, hot cousin, cement mixer, family secrets, "Dance of the Sugar Plum Fairy," sex on clean sheets, fresh aloe, ash blonde, locket, face mask, blank paper, "bruisable," goose down, tetanus shot, glazed clay, vintage Volvo, mink stole, torpedo, Adderall, neti pot, RIP Paul Walker, topiary, bocce, moonlight, shore bird, clean shave, beach towel, cloud waltz, bouffant, the Body of Christ, Fluct Sigrid, pool hair, fancy tracksuit, Jane Lynch, Sunday best, Tide Pods, calfskin gloves, glass candy bowl, candelabra, doll hair, day drunk nap, gold chain, longbow, shipwrecked, post-swim sunbath, star power, opal, field hockey, fiddlehead, cartwheel, catamaran, lemongrass slap, cornbread batter, close shave, Clarice Lispector, mica, Tilda Swinton, storm drain, eucalyptus through the fog, colloidal silver, Nico, thick braid, August haze, egg skin, Capri Sun, plane landing, white fur coat, jacuzzi, warheads, crudité, lady slipper, pool boy, candy wrapper, flip flops, fresh manicure, Seal+Heidi 2005, raw squash, bluffs, porch swing, night swim, *Vanilla Sky*, matriarchy, sun-bleached bones, hemp, sand, tropical cabana, craggy rock, turquoise, dandelion, opal, spring evening, meeting place, river rocks, heiress, jade, sea air, abalone, landline, feathered hair, Chrysler, snakeskin, beautician, glue gun, pedal pushers, houseboat, trophy wife, treasure chest, horse hair brush, sun showers, ear lobe, egg wash, "the Pieta," water wings, cupid's bow, manzanita, Vespa, long silk skirt, sick kiss, winter rose, waders, record brush, best friend crush, sourdough starter, No.2 pencil, walled garden, secret neck tattoo, southern belle, areola, seersucker, shopping spree, "back massager," mirror selfie, feather boa, baby toe, sleepover, fairy dust, hula hoop, fortune teller, Dita Von Teese, IKEA, bosom friends, stained glass, gal pal, lipstick smear, anklet, panty line, Sun In, Skip-It, Evan Rachel Wood, body wave, second base, Fisher-Price swing set, dappled sunlight, navel, salmon skin, pinched nerve, pregnant, light show, lizard tongue, cool mom, daddy long legs, popliteal, wrap around porch, starlet, "she noticed me!," freckles, Seurat paintings, bird feeders, grass on white pants, suck and blow, thigh highs, jewel beetle, juice box, Tank Girl, bleachers, nectar, Calpico, home aquarium, shimmer, plant food, golf ball, balloon static, wooden racket, fat bumblebee, big hickey, bottom lip, Connie Britton, clean comforter, femme 4 femme, A/C blast, Nair, newborn, tennis court, surface tension, Sunday gossip, Deer Isle, ballpoint, hand fan, Oscar Wilde, secret drawer, YKK, born yesterday, yellow storm cloud, sticky bodies, stretched canvas, whiskey, durian, 1970s kitchen, friendly doctor, ring stain, Blo Pens, Saran wrap dress, tire fire, Korean spa, sal de gusano, sponge paint, João Gilberto, sage cleanse, chancletas, someone playing with your hair, graffiti, crushed velvet, scab to scar, Kashi, rowboat, Coppertone, Donatella, yak butter tea, lamplight, *A Wrinkle in Time*, silent retreat, Lauren Bacall, after dinner walk, sucking on a locket, fervent/ silent crush, erhu, angel hair, high dive, unripe, flag flap, bikini wax, David Hockney, eraser, Zoom Flume, doppelgänger, Alice Coltrane, lucid dream, fight or flight, fish camp, Daryl Hannah, tissue paper flower, *A Trip to the Moon*, manta ray, marimba, wet bathing suit, aqueducts, soft face, Best Day Ever, honey sticks, lionfish, long driveway, Vaseline on the lens, hiccup, sno-cone, Ashley Olsen, bottle rocket, prickly pear, ostrich feather, Edelweiss, maracuya, iguana, mimosa, weed whacker, Lil Yachty, whale spray, brocade, cow skull, scroll, sequoia, cut crystal, *Anne of Green Gables*, *Como la Cigarra*, pheromone trigger, mangosteen, first shave, stub tail, "butt stuff," nailed gloves, sleep set, baby head, circlet, department store floor, mink oil, citrus season, suede and shearling, "damn," dewdrop, Coupé de Ville, gua sha, canopy bed, freshly shaved head, natural pearls, white strawberry, morning dreams, velvet water, erotic fan fiction, silky chestnut haunches, fire crack, Brosnan Bond, menthol wild grass, *Twilight*, wall to wall, summer thunder, silk sheets, Brandy (the singer), scraped knee, fox hunt, bloodlust, wishing fountain, double agent, the Space Needle, Maltese, neckerchief, chicha, needlepoint, chicken on the river, shooting star, mulch, my first period, reflexology, *Rude Boy*, peekaboo;), Virgo rising, romantic gesture, waterslide, plush pillow, Mother's Day, night bonnet, office party, hiding from the chaperone, plaster of paris, mandals, velvet dress, wet mouth, hex, Langston Hughes, your gentle glance, wizard hat, cold spring plunge, Saturn return, volcanic ash, berry picking, hot asphalt, duck hunting, my lover left me, scorched earth, lipstick mark, tell-all, Johannes Vermeer, veneers, uvula, assless chaps, surfboard, fresh wisdom, beaded curtain, rodeo floor, cherry stems, Patsy Cline, moon sign, saudade, Pompei, moss, "Last stop!" Rollerblades, new money, I-69, Burt Reynolds, full bush, jersey sheets, turquoise jewelry, jazz dancer, fresh wax, backhanded. calloused hands, turpentine, dog bite, Nefertiti, talisman, kneepads, whipcrack, can-can, motor oil, secret tunnel, gusano, hot asphalt, dad's office, red leather, the Rosetta Stone, stained glass, Capricorn, zip line, NASCAR, dried blood, femme fatale, smoking gun, Persephone, Salma Hayek, jelly donut, crepe paper, wet rope, red rover, rock climbing, rugby, falconry, dark meat, "Clarice," split lip, Venetian plaster, "let me slip into something a little more…comfortable," socket shock, chaise lounge, makeup sex, Loch Ness, mud puddle, hopscotch, Papa, "dinner's ready!," rug burn, night pond, tights off, pillow marks, sticky fingers, soft nipples, calf's liver, cashmere, Mommy, black sand, suffragette, porcelain elephant, 3 Musketeers, aerial silks, lipstick mark, dust storm, blood oath, Aileen Wuornos, "wax on," gray felt, concha, messy pony, loose pearls, threaded brows, backgammon, a handsome stranger reading a book alone at the bar, sealed letter, Elvira, swollen labia, "there there"

CHAPTER FIVE
CLIMAX

SHOWSTOPPING SPREADS TO SEND YOUR SOULMATES INTO CULINARY ECSTASY

RECIPES

At our restaurant, it is very common for a group of adults to leave behind a massacre—lettuces, sauces, fishbones, and rice strewn about the table (and floor) like an Abstract Expressionist painting. When our customers apologize for making a big mess, we say, "It's what happens when you are eating with gusto!" Whether at a restaurant or an intimate dinner party, we always prefer a little too much food, flowing wine, and stimulating conversation. At the dinner table we create our own culture with its own set of manners. Reaching over, arms crossing, double dipping, talking while eating, all are acceptable. And nothing feels better than eating with our hands, surrounded by people we love. We live for this loss of inhibition. Get swept up in the moment, and the outside world fades away.

Increased heartbeats, heightened tensions, weakened knees. These are the telltale signs of escalating pleasure, and we hope you are ready to go there with us. Enjoy the recipes that follow with an orgy of friends. Some of these dishes, like our tamales, will take a full day to prepare, while others, like the lamb ribs, will come together quickly for an impromptu dinner party. We've even included a "recipe" for a riverside lobster dinner concept in which we guide you through the dos and don'ts of casual outdoor dining.

SOFT RULES FOR DINING TOGETHER

Most things can be eaten with your hands—especially salad

✳

Always save the sauce

✳

Family style is the only style

✳

Talking while eating is OK, just don't hog the conversation

✳

Go ahead, take the last bite— whoever said that was bad manners was wrong!

TAMALE PARTY!

Serves a party!
(makes about 24
tamales)

Mushroom Stock

2 lbs shiitake mushroom
   stems and caps, reserve
   stems for stock and
   caps for filling
5 garlic cloves, crushed
   and peeled
1 Tbsp ground cumin

Filling

6 fresh poblano chiles
1 Tbsp canola oil
2 lbs shiitake mushrooms,
   caps cut lengthwise,
   stems reserved
1 tsp kosher salt
½ Tbsp Aleppo or red
   pepper flakes
1 Tbsp freshly ground
   black pepper
3 bunches scallions,
   thinly sliced, reserve
   1 cup for garnish

Masa Dough

3¾ cups coconut oil
5 Tbsp annatto seeds
15 cups masa harina
   (one 4.4 lb bag)
5 Tbsp kosher salt
5 Tbsp baking powder
1 pack frozen banana
   leaves or fresh
   turmeric leaves

(continues next page)

Tamales are little wrapped gifts that comfort and delight. All over Central and South America, tamales are made by comadres y tias, gathered around the kitchen table, and sold by vendors on the street. And in many other countries and on other continents, dough that is steamed and wrapped in husks or leaves is commonplace, like the Senegalese abala. Most tamales are made by women who have years of experience, so their hands have absorbed the rhythms and knowledge of the process over time. Tamales are resilient and, though the process may seem intimidating at first, there's very little that can go wrong if you've managed to fold them into their banana-leaf packages—practice makes perfect! Tamales are a labor of love and an investment of energy, and you'll need a tamale steamer, perforated double boiler, or stacking bamboo steamer baskets. Set aside a whole afternoon to lovingly wrap and steam them with the help of family and friends. Eat tamales together and send leftovers home with your helpers, and don't forget to freeze a few for yourself.

TO MAKE THE MUSHROOM STOCK: Trim the stems of the mushrooms, setting the caps aside. In a stockpot, cover the stems with 12 cups of water and bring to a boil. Add the garlic and cumin, turn the heat to medium, and simmer until the liquid is reduced to 9 cups of finished stock, about 30 minutes. Measure the final liquid, and if you've overreduced, don't worry, just add a little water as needed. Strain the stock, discarding the solids, and set aside to cool slightly.

TO MAKE THE FILLING: Set a rack 4 to 6 inches from the top of the oven and set the broiler to high. Put the poblanos on a baking sheet and slide them under the hot broiler. Broil, rotating the baking sheet every 2 minutes, until the skin has blackened evenly on all sides, 6 to 10 minutes. Transfer to a medium bowl, quickly cover the bowl with plastic wrap, and let steam to loosen the skin from the flesh.

Meanwhile, in a large skillet over medium heat, warm the canola oil. Add the mushrooms and sauté, seasoning with the salt, pepper flakes, and black pepper as they cook, until tender, 5 to 8 minutes. Once cooled, add the scallions and mix thoroughly.

Peel the poblanos with your fingers by pushing the skin away from you. Cut the poblanos into thin strips then add to the mushroom mixture, stirring to incorporate.

TO MAKE THE MASA DOUGH: In a medium saucepan, combine the coconut oil and annatto seeds and bring to a simmer over low heat. Continue simmering for about 5 minutes, being careful not to let the seeds burn. The oil will slowly become bright red as the seeds release their color. Turn off the heat and strain the oil, discarding the seeds. Let the oil cool.

In a large bowl, whisk together the masa harina, salt, and baking powder.

Silky Tomato Turmeric Salsa

One 28 oz can whole or
    crushed tomatoes
2 Tbsp kosher salt
1½ tsp ground cumin
4 garlic cloves
1 small knob fresh
    turmeric, peeled
3 Tbsp unsalted butter
Cumin-Citrus Yogurt
    (page 146), for
    serving (optional)

Pro Tip:

Put a coin at the bottom of
the steamer. As the water
boils, you will hear the rattle
of the coin as it bangs around
the pot. When the water has
evaporated, the coin will stop
moving—listen for the silence
and add more water to keep
your tamales from burning.

Once the mushroom stock is cool enough to handle, gradually pour it into the masa mixture in 3 to 4 parts, kneading it with your hands until the stock is fully incorporated and a rough and flaky dough forms. Gradually add the annatto-coconut oil in 3 to 4 parts, kneading it with your hands until the oil is fully incorporated and the dough has a glossy sheen. Taste the masa. It should be nicely salted, moist, and smooth in texture—masa should be delicious even when raw. If the masa is too dry or crumbly, add water in ¼ cup increments until desired moisture level is reached. Form the masa into a ball, cover with plastic wrap, and let stand for 30 minutes to allow the moisture and flavors to fully incorporate.

Cut the banana leaves into approximately twenty-five 8 in by 10 in pieces. They don't need to be perfect—find beauty in the imperfection.

Once the masa is finished resting, fold the tamales: Divide the masa dough into twenty-five 6 to 7 oz balls. Put a ball of dough in the center of a piece of banana leaf and press down on it firmly with the flat palm of your hand to create a wide circle 3 to 4 in in diameter. Place 2 to 3 Tbsp of filling in the center of the circle. Holding the exposed part of the banana leaf closest to you, fold it up and over the masa and filling, and then peel the banana leaf away. Repeat this process, folding the four sides of the banana leaf over so that the masa nearly encloses the filling. Once this is done, close the banana leaf for steaming, first by folding the part of the leaf closest to you toward the center, then from the left, followed by the right side, and finally the edge farthest away from you. Repeat to make more tamales.

TO STEAM THE TAMALES: Fill the bottom of a tamale steamer, double boiler, or the pot for a steamer basket with enough water to come just below the steamer. Bring to a boil. Working in batches as needed, arrange the tamales in the steamer, leaving ¼ in gaps in between, and stacking them in several layers. Carefully place the tamale-filled steamer basket above the boiling water. Turn the heat to medium and steam, checking the water level every 20 minutes and adding more as needed, until the masa is fully cooked and loses the grainy quality of raw masa, about 1 hour. Remove from the steamer and keep warm while you cook more tamales. Alternatively, allow the tamales to cool completely then wrap and freeze for up to 6 months. To reheat, place frozen tamales in a steamer basket and steam over boiling water until warm in the center, 20 to 30 minutes.

TO MAKE THE SALSA: In a blender, combine the tomatoes, salt, cumin, garlic, turmeric, and 1 cup of water and blend until smooth, adding more water as needed—the salsa will be fairly loose. Check the salt level. Reserve the butter for serving time. Set aside.

TO SERVE: In a small saucepan over low heat, bring the tomato salsa to a gentle simmer. Add the butter, stirring to incorporate. Carefully open a hot tamale and spoon salsa over the top. Sprinkle with scallions and drizzle with cumin-citrus yogurt if you choose to make it.

MARIA'S PUPUSAS

Serves 4 to 6 (makes 12 pupusas)

Repollo

⅓ cup kosher salt, plus
    more as needed
1 small or ½ large red
    or green cabbage
1 medium yellow onion
2 carrots, grated
2 jalapeños, cut into rounds
½ cup white distilled
    vinegar, plus more
    as needed
1 Tbsp dried oregano

Bean Filling

1 Tbsp neutral oil
1½ cups Abuela's Black
    Beans (page 165) or
    one 12 oz can black
    beans and their liquid
1 tsp kosher salt
1 cup grated mozzarella
    cheese

Masa Dough

3⅓ cups masa harina
    (about 1 lb)
Neutral oil

Silky Tomato Turmeric
    Salsa (page 180)

Maria Romero contains multitudes: She is a Taurus, a chef, a matriarch, El Salvadorian, and truly a wonderful person. We first met her while she was selling pupusas outside of her home, around the corner from the restaurant, and we asked her if she would teach us how to make tortillas. Maria said yes, and she soon became instrumental to our first year in business, with her whole family becoming the backbone of our little operation.

As our business began to grow, so did Maria's desire to cook Salvadoran food for the community. She and her family started selling pupusas at our counter for lunch and on nights when we were closed. Maria is now the proud owner of Casa Latina Pupusas y Mas, just down the road from our restaurant. In honor of Maria and her family, and with her permission, we are sharing her pupusa recipe with you. These soft and gooey cheese-filled pockets of love will leave you craving more. Leftover repollo makes a bright, tangy addition to any meal.

TO MAKE THE REPOLLO: In a medium pot bring 4 qts of water to a boil over high heat. Add the salt.

Meanwhile, cut the cabbage into quarters, removing and discarding the hard white center. Using a mandoline, cut the cabbage lengthwise into ¼ in thick pieces. Repeat with the onion. Reserve about a quarter of the onion slices for the bean filling. Add the remaining onion and the cabbage to the boiling water. Turn off the heat and let stand until the cabbage is soft, 8 to 10 minutes. Drain and transfer to a large bowl. Add the carrots, jalapeños, vinegar, and oregano and mix thoroughly. Season with more salt and vinegar as needed. Repollo should be tangy, bright, and nicely salted. Until ready to use, it can be stored in an airtight container in the refrigerator for up to 5 days.

TO MAKE THE BEAN FILLING: In a small pot over medium-high heat, warm the oil. Add the reserved onion and cook until charred, 8 to 10 minutes. Transfer the onion to a blender, leaving the oil in the pot. Add the black beans and their liquid to the blender and blend until smooth. Transfer the bean mixture to the pot with the reserved oil, add the salt, and fry over medium heat, stirring until the beans begin to bubble and pull away from the edges of the pot, about 5 minutes. Transfer to a small bowl and let cool completely.

In a small bowl, combine the mozzarella and 2 tsp of water and use your hands to mash them together until the water is absorbed and the cheese has a paste-like texture.

When the beans are cool to the touch, add the cheese and mix until well incorporated.

TO MAKE THE MASA DOUGH: Put the masa harina flour into a large bowl. Add 3 cups of water and mix with your hands until well incorporated—the dough should be smooth and pliable but not sticky. If your masa is too dry and crumbling or cracking, add a splash of water. If it is too wet and sticking to your hands, add a dash of masa harina. Divide the dough into 12 pieces, each slightly larger than a golf ball.

Put a few tablespoons of neutral oil in a small bowl to oil your fingers as needed to avoid sticking or tearing. Alternatively, a bowl of ice water works, too. Line a baking sheet with parchment paper.

TO MAKE THE PUPUSAS: Flatten a ball of dough between your hands, forming a circle about 3 in in diameter. Hold the flattened dough in one hand, slightly cupping your hand to create a small cup-like indent in the center of the dough. Place 1 to 2 Tbsp of the bean filling in the center of the dough. Oil or wet your fingers as needed and use them to bring the outer edges of the masa dough toward the middle, pressing the opposite sides together to form a pouch. If there is excess dough at the tip, pull it off and set it to the side—you can use it later to form more pupusas. Once the edges are thoroughly sealed, begin flattening the pouch by alternating it between your hands, patty-cake style, until it's about ½ in thick and 4 inches in diameter. Patch tears with scraps of masa. Any gaps in the surface of the dough will produce crispy bits of cheese when you cook them—they're our favorite kind of oops! Put the shaped pupusas on the parchment-lined sheet tray and repeat to make more pupusas.

Be patient with yourself. Any complicated technique takes time to master and your hands have a lot of learning to do. Your last round of pupusas will undoubtedly look better than your first. That's okay! The next time you make these they will come out even better. Muscle memory grows with time and practice. Love yourself as you learn, it's the only way you'll get better.

When you are ready to cook your pupusas, set a cast-iron skillet, griddle, or nonstick pan over medium-high heat. Lightly oil the cooking surface. When the pan is nice and hot, add as many pupusas as will fit comfortably without touching and cook, flipping every 2 minutes, until mottled honey-brown on the top and bottom, 6 to 8 minutes total. Repeat to cook more pupusas. Keep the pupusas warm by tenting them with foil. Serve immediately with a generous portion of repollo and a douse of tomato sauce (best heated first). Leftover repollo makes a bright, tangy addition to any meal.

Order! Order in the Court!

In a conventional wine tasting, wines progress from light to heavy, from sparkling varieties to heavy reds. But this isn't our way! Instead, serve your wines in the order of how much you want to savor them. We have felt a specific type of regret at having served a Special Occasion bottle to friends when a more casual wine would have done fine. Sharing a Special Occasion bottle (you spent Special Money on it, or you've been saving it for a rainy day) is important, and once you've enjoyed sharing two bottles, the third one may feel less special. There comes a point in the night when the type of wine begins to matter less! Our advice is to start with the wine you're most excited about, so you will enjoy it with the most presence of mind—and palate—that you'll have that night.

STUFFED CABBAGE ROLLS

Serves 3 to 6 (makes 15 rolls)

Sauce

3 Tbsp unsalted butter
1 large yellow onion, minced
4 garlic cloves, minced
¼ cup peeled and grated carrot
1 Tbsp kosher salt
1 tsp freshly ground pink, green, or black peppercorns
1 tsp peeled and grated fresh turmeric
½ tsp ground cumin
One 15 oz can tomato purée

Cabbage Rolls

Kosher salt
1 head savoy cabbage

Filling

¾ cup white jasmine rice
¼ cup red or yellow lentils
3 Tbsp unsalted butter
1½ cups chopped shiitake, cremini, oyster, or maitake mushrooms
¾ cup peeled and grated carrot
4 garlic cloves, minced
¼ cup chopped dried sour cherries, prunes, or apricots
½ tsp peeled and grated fresh turmeric (or ¼ tsp ground)
1 Tbsp peeled and grated ginger

Stuffed cabbage is another one of those dishes you'll find scattered across the globe. Versions exist in every far-reaching corner, from Ukraine to China to Ecuador to Azerbaijan. Each country, not to mention each household, has its own special interpretation that is absolutely *the best*. Ours is vegetarian and features sour cherries, which bring a cheeky sweetness to the final dish. This recipe works well with many different varieties of mushroom, so explore your grocer's selection. We recommend making the sauce and the filling a day or two in advance.

TO MAKE THE SAUCE: In a large shallow saucepan with a lid or a Dutch oven, melt the butter over medium heat. Reserve three-quarters of the onion to make the filling then add the rest to the pan and sauté until translucent, about 5 minutes. Add the garlic and carrot and sauté, being careful not to burn the garlic, until soft, about 3 minutes. Add the salt, pepper, turmeric, and cumin and sauté for 2 minutes then add the tomato purée and ½ cup of water and bring to a simmer. Continue cooking until the spices permeate the sauce, about 6 minutes. Remove from the heat and set aside.

TO MAKE THE CABBAGE ROLLS: Bring a large pot of generously salted water to a roaring boil. In a large bowl, make an ice bath of half ice and half water. Line a baking sheet with clean kitchen towels.

Separate the largest leaves from the cabbage—you will need about 15 leaves (use leftover cabbage to make repollo; see page 182). Working in batches, add the cabbage leaves to the boiling water and blanch until they turn bright green and soft, about 2 minutes. Immediately plunge into the ice bath to stop the cooking process and maintain the bright green color. Transfer to the towel-lined baking sheet and let dry. Repeat to blanch the remaining cabbage leaves. Keep the hot water.

TO MAKE THE FILLING: Bring the pot of water back to a boil. Add the rice and lentils and blanch until soft but still al dente, about 5 minutes. Pour through a fine-mesh strainer and run under cold water to stop the cooking process. Transfer to a large bowl.

In a medium sauté pan over medium heat, melt the butter. Add the reserved minced onion, along with the mushrooms, carrot, garlic, sour cherries, turmeric, and ginger, and sauté until soft, about 6 to 8 minutes. If the cherries clump together, loosen them with your hands to evenly distribute.

Add the cumin, paprika, and salt and stir to incorporate. Add to the rice and lentil mixture. Season with salt.

Remove and discard the stiff inner stalk from each blanched cabbage leaf, keeping the leaves intact—each one will have a slit up the middle. Place

2 tsp ground cumin
1 Tbsp sweet paprika
1 Tbsp kosher salt

Greek yogurt or sour
    cream, for serving
Chopped dill, scallions,
    cilantro, or parsley,
    for serving

2 to 3 tablespoons of the filling in the center of a leaf, right above the cut slit, and begin to roll up the leaf by first folding in the sides, and then wrapping the leaf tightly around the filling from the top to bottom as you would roll a burrito. Repeat to make more cabbage rolls, adjusting the amount of filling as needed. As you go, nestle the cabbage rolls, seam side down, in the tomato sauce. When they're all rolled up, cozy and nested in the tomato sauce, bring to a gentle simmer over medium heat then turn the heat as low as possible, cover, and cook for 30 minutes. Gently lift a roll out of the sauce to test if the rice is tender; if the grains remain toothsome, cook for 5 more minutes. Serve hot, with a dollop of cold Greek yogurt or sour cream and a garden of fresh herbs.

MOJO CHICKEN

Serves 4 to 6

Special equipment:
Spice grinder, high-speed
blender, resting rack

Chicken
One 4 to 5 lb chicken
2 Tbsp kosher salt

Achiote Paste
¼ cup annatto seeds
3 Tbsp paprika
1 Tbsp coriander seeds
1 Tbsp allspice berries
1 tsp cumin seeds
1 tsp black peppercorns
2 cinnamon sticks or 2 tsp
    ground cinnamon
1 cup extra-virgin olive oil
3 Tbsp kosher salt
20 garlic cloves

Yellow Sauce
⅓ cup ají amarillo paste or
    1 orange bell pepper
    and 1 habanero pepper
5 garlic cloves
Zest of 1 orange
2 Tbsp freshly squeezed
    orange juice
1 Tbsp kosher salt
1 tsp lime juice
1 tsp turmeric
1 cup Greek yogurt

This is our take on classic Peruvian rotisserie chicken, which always comes with the choice of yellow or green sauces. Here, we reveal our best kept saucy secrets. In our restaurant, this dish has survived several reimaginings under the same name. And while this recipe has very little to do with traditional versions of mojo sauce, we've kept the name with every revision because almost everyone pronounces it the Anglo-Saxon way with a hard "j" à la Muddy Waters, rather than the Castellano pronunciation with a soft "j" sound like mo-ho. Instead of correcting their pronunciation, we've chosen to play along because, at the end of the day, mojo means magic.

We think the flavors of our earthy achiote paste (use leftovers to flavor soups and dishes like our Llapingachos, page 132), combined with the floral and herbal notes from the sauces, are magical. The ají amarillo paste used in the yellow sauce is made from a Peruvian yellow pepper and can be tricky to source, so we've included an alternative. Make the sauces and paste a day in advance, so the flavors bloom, and be sure to salt the chicken overnight, which produces extra crispy skin. If you prefer, you can ask your butcher to spatch-cock the chicken.

One Day Ahead

TO MAKE THE CHICKEN: Put the chicken on a cutting board with the breast side down and the wings closest to you. Using a sharp boning knife or poultry shears, cut along both sides of the backbone to remove it (freeze the backbone and use it to fortify chicken broth). Flip the bird breast-side up and press down firmly to break the breastbone until the chicken lays flat. Pat dry with paper towels and place breast-side up on a baking sheet. Generously and thoroughly salt the chicken all over. Tuck each wingtip behind the breast and refrigerate, uncovered, overnight.

TO MAKE THE ACHIOTE PASTE: In a small pan over low heat, toast the annatto, paprika, coriander, allspice, cumin, peppercorns, and cinnamon until fragrant, about 4 minutes. Transfer to a high-speed blender then add the olive oil, salt, and garlic and blend until smooth. The ideal texture will have very little graininess, and the spices should be finely ground. (Alternatively, grind the spices into a fine powder in a spice grinder then put in a bowl, add the olive oil, salt, and garlic, and whisk to combine.) Transfer to an airtight container and refrigerate until ready to use or for up to 3 months.

TO MAKE THE YELLOW SAUCE WITH AJÍ AMARILLO: Blend all ingredients, except the yogurt, in a blender on high until smooth and thoroughly combined. (If using the orange bell pepper, broil for 6 to 10 minutes, until the skin begins to lift off the flesh. Then allow it to cool slightly before peeling

Green Sauce

1 cup chopped cilantro

½ cup unsweetened full-fat
   coconut milk

½ cup mayonnaise

Zest and juice of 2 limes

4 garlic cloves, smashed
   and peeled

1 or 2 fresh serrano chiles,
   seeds removed

1 Tbsp kosher salt

For Serving

1 bunch scallions
   (optional)

Fragrant Chile Oil
   (page 38)

Abuela's Aromatic Rice
   (page 164)

Abuela's Black Beans
   (page 165)

Lime wedges

and removing the seeds and blending with the other ingredients, including the habanero pepper). Transfer to a medium-size bowl, add the yogurt, and fold to incorporate. Season with salt. Transfer to an airtight container and refrigerate until ready to use or for up to a week.

TO MAKE THE GREEN SAUCE: In a blender, combine the cilantro, coconut milk, mayonnaise, lime zest and juice, garlic, serrano chiles, and salt and blend until smooth and bright green. Transfer to an airtight container and refrigerate until ready to use or for up to a week.

The Next Day

Set a rack in the middle of the oven and preheat the oven to 350°F. Set a wire rack in a baking sheet.

Remove the chicken from the refrigerator at least 1 hour before roasting, so it can come to room temperature. Rub the chicken with ¼ cup of achiote paste and salt liberally, covering all exposed skin as well as the nether regions.

Put the chicken on the rack set in the baking sheet and bake in the center of the oven for 30 minutes. Raise the oven temperature to 450°F and roast until the top of the chicken is a deep reddish brown, the internal temperature reaches 165°F on a meat thermometer, and the juices run clear, about 10 minutes. Continue roasting in 5-minute increments as needed. Transfer to a cutting board and rest for 10 minutes. Cut the chicken into pieces for serving.

If desired, char the scallions in a large pan over high heat until wilted. Season lightly with salt.

TO SERVE: Spread the yellow and green sauces in generous swooshes going in opposite directions on a serving platter. Place the chicken pieces on top, drizzle with chile oil, and sprinkle with the charred scallions, if using. Serve with the rice, beans, and lime wedges.

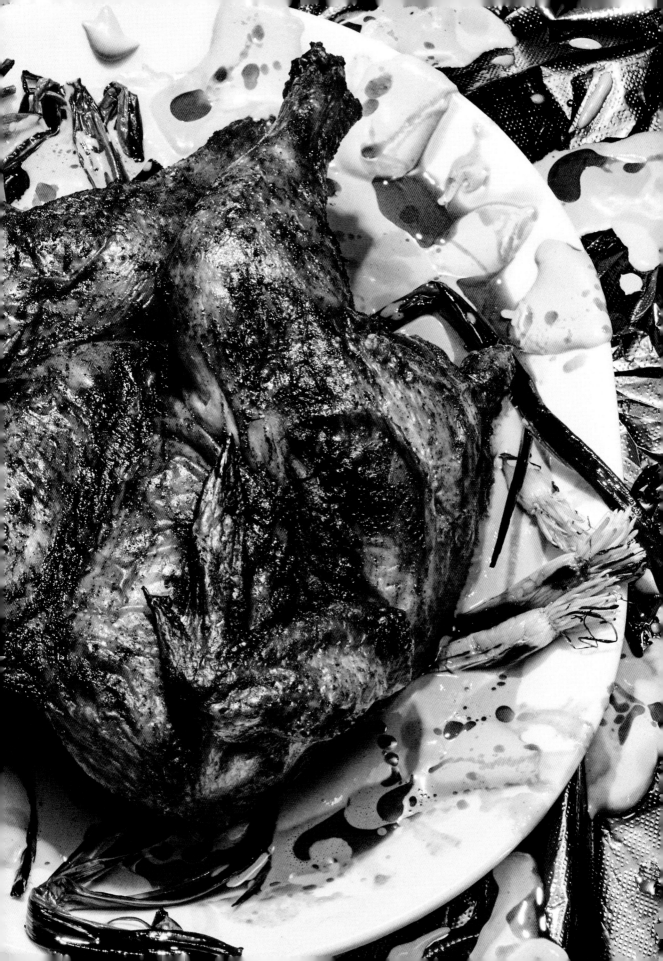

DULCE DE LECHE PORK WITH TAMARIND DIPPING SAUCE

Serves 4 to 6

Dulce de Leche

One 14 oz can sweetened
  condensed milk

Pork

8 oz tamarind pulp
2 cups boiling water
6 garlic cloves, minced
2 tsp ground turmeric
1 tsp ground allspice
½ tsp freshly ground
  white pepper
¼ cup fish sauce, plus
  more as needed
3 to 5 lbs pork neck bones

Dipping Sauce

1 shallot, cut into thin
  half moons
¼ cup freshly squeezed
  lime juice
2 Tbsp fish sauce
½ cup chopped cashews
2 Tbsp granulated sugar
1 tsp freshly ground
  black pepper

Chopped dill, basil,
  cilantro, or mint,
  for serving

This dish is inspired by the pork collar served at the wonderful Thai restaurant Night + Market in Los Angeles, where they marinate pork in condensed milk. Fascinated by the idea, we experimented with dulce de leche (caramelized milk) and fell in love with its honey-like flavor. In our recipe, the sweetness of the dulce de leche is balanced by the fattiness of the meat and the acidic brightness of the tamarind dipping sauce. The rich marbling of pork collar, due to its proximity to the fatty jowl of the pig, lands this cut in the unctuous world of oxtail and ribs. If pork collar, also known as pork neck, is not available, use pork ribs or shoulder, but lower the oven temperature to 300°F and increase the cooking time to about 3 hours. Serve with a side of Abuela's Aromatic Rice (page 164) or What's in the Fridge Chef's Tiger Salad (page 120).

TO MAKE THE DULCE DE LECHE: Remove and discard the paper label from the can of sweetened condensed milk and put the can, unopened, in a medium saucepan. Add enough water to cover the can and bring to a boil over medium heat. Continue boiling for 1 to 1½ hours. Using tongs, carefully remove the can from the water and let cool completely before opening.

TO MAKE THE PORK: In a medium bowl, combine the tamarind and boiling water and set aside for 10 to 15 minutes.

Meanwhile, in a small bowl, combine the minced garlic, turmeric, allspice, and white pepper.

Once the tamarind is cool enough to handle, pull it apart by hand. The fruity flesh should melt into the liquid; discard the seed pods and any stringy material. Push the tamarind liquid through a fine-mesh sieve into a medium bowl. Pour one half of the liquid into the turmeric mixture; reserve the other half for the dipping sauce. Add the dulce de leche and whisk to incorporate. Taste. The marinade should be sweet, salty, and tangy, with warming spices in the background. Season with additional fish sauce as needed. Pour the marinade over the neck bones, cover, and refrigerate overnight.

TO MAKE THE DIPPING SAUCE: In a small bowl, combine the shallots, lime juice, fish sauce, tamarind liquid reserved from the marinade, cashews, sugar, and pepper. Set aside for 1 hour before serving.

At least 1 hour before roasting the pork, remove it from the refrigerator and let it come to room temperature. Preheat the oven to 350°F. In a roasting pan, enclose the pork neck bones in a foil tent without crowding them. Roast until tender and juicy, about 45 minutes. Rest for 20 minutes before serving. Garnish with herbs and serve with dipping sauce.

CURRY LEAF LAMB RIBS

Serves 2 to 4

Lamb
½ oz fresh curry leaves
3 Tbsp kosher salt
2 to 3 lbs French-cut
  lamb ribs

Lime Pickle Yogurt
1 cup full-fat Greek
  yogurt
¼ cup lime pickle,
  finely chopped
Kosher salt

Plumped Raisin Relish
½ cup golden raisins
¼ cup Chile Vinegar
  (page 39)
1 tsp kosher salt
1 shallot, cut into
  thin slivers
1 Tbsp extra-virgin
  olive oil

Lamb ribs are one of our favorite cuts of meat—moist, succulent, and full of flavor. Plus, they cook quickly, making them a great choice for a weeknight meal or to impress a crowd with ease. Here, we use curry leaves to impart their wildly pungent flavor, both in a rub and as a super delicious crispy garnish. Lime pickle and curry leaves can be purchased at Indian grocery stores or online. Lime pickle comes in two styles, spicy (our preference) and sweet. You can use either one for this recipe. The lamb needs to be started a day in advance but you can also make the yogurt and raisin salad a day ahead.

One Day Ahead

TO MAKE THE LAMB: Set aside a handful of curry leaves for garnish, if desired. Pound the remaining curry leaves using a mortar and pestle or pulse in a food processor. Add the salt and mix to fully combine.

Trim excess fat from the ribs as needed. With a sharp knife, score the remaining fat to create cross-hatching, being careful to only cut the top layer of fat and not the flesh—this will help maximize rendering. Coat both sides of the ribs with the curry salt. Refrigerate overnight.

TO MAKE THE YOGURT: In a small bowl, combine the yogurt and lime pickle. Season with salt, cover, and refrigerate until ready to use or for up to 1 day.

TO MAKE THE RAISIN SALAD: In a small saucepan, bring the raisins, chile vinegar, and salt to a boil. Turn off the heat and let cool. Add the shallots and olive oil and mix to fully combine. Set aside for 20 minutes before serving or cover and refrigerate for up to 1 day.

The Next Day

At least 1 hour before roasting the lamb, remove it from the refrigerator and let it come to room temperature. Set a rack in the middle of the oven and preheat the oven to 450°F. Line a baking sheet with aluminum foil.

Put the lamb on the foil-lined baking sheet and roast in the middle of the oven for 12 minutes. Rotate the baking sheet and continue roasting until the internal temperature reaches 130 to 140°F on a meat thermometer for medium-rare or 140 to 145°F for medium, the top of the lamb is crispy, and the fat glistens happily, about 5 more minutes. Put the lamb under the broiler for 3 to 5 minutes as needed. Transfer the meat to a cutting board and let rest for 6 to 10 minutes.

TO SERVE: Smear generous spoonfuls of the lime pickle yogurt on individual plates. Using a sharp knife, carve the lamb by cutting between each exposed rib bone. Place ribs, one crossed over the other, on top of the yogurt on each plate. Serve with a heaping amount of the raisin salad. Don't forget to nibble the crisped fat off the bones at the dinner table!

BITTERSWEET BEEF SHANK WITH CHARRED ONION PETALS

Serves 4 to 6

Beef

½ cup kosher salt, plus more if needed

3 lbs whole beef shank

2 star anise pods

2 dried pasilla or ancho chiles, stems removed

1 dried chile de árbol

1 tsp cumin seeds

1 Tbsp ground coffee

1 tsp urfa biber

2 tsp cacao powder

Canola oil, for cooking

3 small onions, quartered

2 cups red wine

3 cups beef or chicken stock or water

2 carrots, peeled and cut into 1 in pieces

1 head of garlic, halved across the middle

1 orange, quartered

4 sprigs thyme

1 cup freshly squeezed orange juice

1 to 2 Tbsp unsalted butter

1 Tbsp toasted white sesame seeds

Pinch of sugar, if needed

Black Sesame Tahini

1 cup black sesame seeds

2 Tbsp toasted sesame oil

⅓ to ½ cup extra-virgin olive oil

This dish is the epitome of dinner party sexiness. The sauce lands somewhere between mole negro and bordelaise and provides deep pools of flavor for the meat as it falls off the bone. While we prefer whole beef shank for its star-quality, beef cheeks, oxtail, or brisket would work, too. If time is on your side, season the meat overnight and start braising before you get too hungry, as this dish requires three hours to cook. The homemade tahini is a deep black, sexy, unctuous paste—you'll want to slather it on toast and drizzle it on desserts too.

TO MAKE THE BEEF: Sprinkle the salt generously on all sides of the beef shank and set aside.

In a Dutch oven over medium heat, toast the star anise, both chiles, and the cumin seeds until fragrant, about 2 minutes. Transfer to a blender or coffee grinder, add the ground coffee and urfa biber, and grind into a medium-fine powder. Transfer to a medium bowl, add the cacao powder, and stir to combine. Generously dust the spice mixture on all sides of the beef. Let stand at room temperature for 1 hour or refrigerate overnight.

TO MAKE THE BLACK SESAME TAHINI: In a medium skillet over low heat, toast the black sesame seeds until fragrant, about 5 minutes. Transfer to a high-speed blender or food processor and pulse until the seeds begin to crumble and form a rough paste. Add the sesame oil and blend until a smooth paste forms, gradually adding more oil, 1 to 2 Tbsp at a time, as needed if the seeds aren't turning into a paste—tahini takes time to come together, so be patient. The tahini can be stored in an airtight container for up to 1 month in the refrigerator.

If the beef is refrigerated, at least 1 hour before braising, remove it from the refrigerator and let it come to room temperature. Preheat the oven to 300°F.

In a Dutch oven, heat a few tablespoons of canola oil over high heat until nearly smoking. Add the onions and char, turning as needed, until black on both cut sides, about 8 minutes. Remove the onions and set aside.

Wipe out the Dutch oven. Add fresh oil and heat over high heat until nearly smoking. Working in batches, add the beef shank and sear, turning as needed, until deep brown, about 2 minutes on each side. Remove the shank and set aside. Add the wine and deglaze the Dutch oven, scraping any browned bits with a wooden spoon and allowing the wine to reduce slightly. Add the stock, carrots, garlic, orange quarters, thyme, and half of the charred onion. Nestle the shank in the vegetables and citrus. Cover, put in the oven, and cook for 2½ hours. Check the meat for tenderness and continue cooking until the beef is very tender and slipping off the bone, about 30 more minutes.

Remove the shank and braised vegetables from the Dutch oven and keep warm. Pour the braising liquid through a fine-mesh sieve. Transfer the strained braising liquid to a medium saucepan, add the orange juice, and bring to a boil over medium-high heat. Turn the heat to medium-low and simmer until reduced to a glossy, drippy liquid, about 20 minutes. Use a spoon to remove fat from the top. Add the butter and tahini and stir to incorporate. Season with a pinch of salt or sugar. Return the shank to the Dutch oven and spoon the sauce on top.

TO SERVE: Separate the reserved charred onion quarters into petals and arrange on individual plates, along with the braised vegetables. Place the shank on top, drizzle with the sauce, and sprinkle with toasted sesame seeds.

How Do I Know If a Wine Is Tannic?

When you taste a wine, pay attention to the actual texture on your tongue. Does it feel like a sudden case of cottonmouth? Think about the last time you had a cup of black tea that was too strong and how that felt. Do you notice any similar sensations? A common misconception is that a wine is either tannic or not; tannins exist more on a scale than as binary, just like us ;) A wine can range in tannin levels from high to medium or low and anywhere in between. The classic pairing of big, tannic red wines and beef exists for a scientific reason! The enzymes in our saliva are not the only things that tannin can break down. When you drink a tannic wine with a dense animal protein like beef shank, the tannins help the meat break down into something more manageable for your body to digest before it reaches your stomach.

FISHBONE SOUP

Serves 4 to 6

2 small, white-fleshed
    fish, about 1 lb each,
    gutted and scaled
½ cup (1 stick) unsalted
    butter
1 onion, cut into thin
    half moons
12 garlic cloves, smashed
    and peeled
2 celery sticks, cut on a
    bias into 1 in pieces
1 carrot, peeled and cut
    into 1 in chunks
½ kabocha or acorn
    squash, halved, seeds
    removed, and cut into
    1 in thick half moons
3 bay leaves
Kosher salt
3 cups roughly chopped
    hearty greens, such
    as savoy cabbage,
    mustard greens, or
    tatsoi
1 lemon, halved,
    for serving
1 cup chopped dill,
    for serving

This rustic, one-pot meal is designed to please a crowd or soothe your soul on a quiet night in. Hot, spicy, and nourishing, it is the perfect antidote to a wicked hangover. It can also give you a hearty kick out of whatever malaise you may be feeling. Allow yourself to be comforted by the warm bowl. Experience the steam as it permeates your orifices—breathe in deeply, exhale, and acknowledge your oneness with the universe. We are all in this together. Let your newfound mindfulness bring awareness to the fact that there are fishbones in this dish, so take care.

At least 30 minutes before cooking, remove the fish from the refrigerator and let it come to room temperature.

In a stockpot over medium-low heat, melt the butter. Add the onion and sauté until translucent, about 4 minutes. Add the garlic and sauté for 2 minutes. Add 12 cups of water, along with the celery, carrot, squash, bay leaves, and 2 Tbsp of salt, and bring to a boil. Turn the heat to low and simmer until the vegetables are tender but still hold their shape, about 30 minutes.

Meanwhile, using a very sharp knife, cut each fish crosswise into thirds, so you have head, middle, and tail pieces. Generously season the fish pieces with salt and gently place them in the soup, on top of the bed of vegetables and so the liquid just barely covers them. Tuck the greens around the fish, cover, and gently simmer until the greens are wilted and the fish is cooked through, about 10 more minutes. Season with salt.

TO SERVE: Divide the fish and vegetables among soup bowls. Ladle in the broth, spritz with lemon juice, and sprinkle generously with dill.

Note:
For faint-of-heart friends, one could remove the fish and pick the flesh off the bones and serve sans head, but gently remind them that they are missing out on the primal connection to flesh and sustenance.

SEAFOOD MOQUECA

Serves 6 to 8

Cashew-Coconut Cream

½ cup unsweetened
    coconut milk
2 Tbsp raw unsalted
    cashews

Moqueca

1 lb mussels
½ lb clams
1 lb firm white-fleshed
    fish fillet, cut into
    2 or 3 in chunks
Juice of 1 lime
Kosher salt
1 Tbsp coconut oil
2 tsp annatto seeds
1 medium yellow onion,
    cut into large dice
2 cups crushed tomatoes
3 garlic cloves, minced
1 red bell pepper,
    seeded, stemmed,
    and cut into rings
1 small fresh Fresno,
    jalapeño, or serrano
    chile, cut into rings
1 bunch cilantro,
    leaves and stems,
    chopped
¼ cup chopped scallions
1 Tbsp sweet paprika
4 cups fish, shrimp,
    chicken, or
    vegetable stock
One 14 oz can
    unsweetened
    coconut milk
¼ cup fish sauce, plus
    more as needed
½ lb shrimp, peeled
    and deveined

2 Tbsp Shrimp Butter (page
    161) or unsalted butter
1 Tbsp Fragrant Chile Oil
    (page 38)
2 limes, cut into wedges,
    for garnish

Silky, abundant, and romantic (just like us), this seafood stew is perfect for an opulent date night or dinner party. The history of moqueca, however, should not be taken lightly, as it is a dish that embodies the complicated history of the Atlantic slave trade in Brazil. The exact origin of the dish is contested, but historians have located it in the southeastern Bahia region of Brazil, as well as in its neighboring state of Espírito Santo, where the dish varies slightly. Moqueca is traditionally prepared with dende oil made from the pulp of the fruit of the African oil palm, an essential ingredient in the cuisine of West Africa that was brought to Brazil on Portuguese slave ships. The oil's distinctive flavor and texture is impossible to replicate, but we use annatto seeds to mimic its color. If you have access to dende oil, use it. This dish should have a deep, silky seafood flavor with subtle sweetness from the coconut and peppers. Serve it with Abuela's Aromatic Rice (page 164) or crusty bread.

TO MAKE THE CASHEW-COCONUT CREAM: In a blender, combine the coconut milk and cashews and blend on high till smooth and creamy. Set aside in the refrigerator for up to a week.

TO MAKE THE MOQUECA: Clean the mussels and clams in cold water, removing any dirt and the beards from the mussels. Season the fish with lime juice and salt. Set aside in separate bowls.

In a heavy-bottomed pot over low heat, melt the coconut oil. Add the annatto seeds and gently cook until the oil turns bright red, about 4 minutes. Use a slotted spoon to remove the seeds; discard. Add the onions, turn the heat to medium, and sauté until translucent, about 4 minutes. Add the tomatoes, garlic, red bell pepper, chile, half of the cilantro, the scallions, and the paprika and cook until the vegetables turn soft, about 8 minutes. Stir in the stock and coconut milk. Gradually add the fish sauce, a splash at a time, as needed. Cover and bring to a boil. Add the clams, cover, and steam until they begin to open, about 5 minutes. Add the mussels, cover, and steam until they open, about 3 minutes. Add the fish and shrimp, cover, and steam until just cooked through, about 3 minutes. Stir in the shrimp butter.

TO SERVE: Divide the moqueca among bowls, sprinkle with the remaining cilantro, and drizzle with the cashew-coconut cream and fragrant chile oil. Garnish with lime wedges.

CHARRED OCTOPUS IN THE INK OF ITS COUSIN

Serves 4

Octopus

1 red onion, quartered
1 orange, quartered
One 1 to 2 lb octopus, thawed and rinsed
½ bunch cilantro, leaves and stems
¼ cup coriander seeds
1½ cups red wine
1 Tbsp neutral oil

Potatoes

1 lb small Yukon Gold or fingerling potatoes, halved
1 Tbsp extra-virgin olive oil
2 tsp kosher salt
1 tsp smoked paprika

Vinaigrette

Zest and juice of 1 lemon
1 garlic clove, finely grated
2 Tbsp extra-virgin olive oil
2 Tbsp squid ink (optional)
1 tsp red wine vinegar
1 tsp smoked paprika
Sea salt

Salad

1 head bitter lettuce, such as radicchio, escarole, or both
1 cup mixed fresh herbs
½ red onion, cut into thin half moons

Optional

½ recipe Lovage Aioli (page 217)

Octopus can be hard to find, but it's one of our favorite proteins. (A seven-year-old friend of ours loves it because, she says, "It tastes just like chicken."). Call your fishmonger ahead of time to ask if they have octopus in stock or can special order it. Often, it comes frozen, which is actually good—freezing makes it more tender, and we *love* tenderness. Squid ink for the vinaigrette may be hard to find too, but it can be ordered online or found at fancy specialty food stores. We also give you permission to forego the ink! While sourcing may require time and patience, this dish will not disappoint!

TO MAKE THE OCTOPUS: Preheat the oven to 300°F.

Put the onion and orange quarters in a Dutch oven, and put the octopus on top. Add the cilantro and coriander, followed by the red wine. If the octopus isn't completely covered, add enough water until it is fully submerged in liquid. Cover, put in the oven, and cook until the octopus is easily pierced with a fork, about 3 hours.

Remove the octopus from the Dutch oven and set aside to cool on a tray. Pour the braising liquid through a fine-mesh sieve, discarding any solids. Measure 1 cup of the strained liquid and set aside; discard any extra liquid.

TO MAKE THE POTATOES: Raise the oven temperature to 450°F. On a large baking sheet, toss the potatoes with the olive oil, salt, and smoked paprika. Roast, tossing occasionally, until the potatoes are crisp and golden brown, 25 to 30 minutes. Keep warm.

TO MAKE THE VINAIGRETTE: In a small pot over medium heat, bring the reserved braising liquid to a boil. Turn the heat to medium and simmer until reduced by half, about 20 minutes. Set aside to cool. Add the lemon zest and juice, garlic, olive oil, squid ink, if using, vinegar, and smoked paprika and whisk to combine. Let stand for 20 minutes at room temperature, so that the garlic can bloom. Season with salt.

When the octopus has cooled, remove the head and cut it into rings. Discard the hard piece in the center known as the beak. Cut the tentacles into evenly sized pieces.

In a cast-iron skillet over high heat, warm 1 tablespoon of neutral oil. Working in batches, add the octopus pieces and char, turning as needed, until crispy on all sides, about 4 minutes on each side. Remove the octopus from the skillet and keep warm while you char the remaining octopus.

TO SERVE: Arrange generous handfuls of crispy potatoes on individual plates. In a large bowl, toss the bitter lettuce, fresh herbs, and red onion with some of the vinaigrette. Place a handful of the salad on top of the potatoes

on each plate—try to create some height and drama! Gingerly place the octopus on the greens. Confidently drizzle more vinaigrette on the octopus. Eat with a fork and steak knife or gobble up barehanded. Your hands will stain from the dark black ink. It's sexy. Enjoy it :)

HIBISCUS GLAZED PRAWNS

Serves 6

Shrimp

2 Tbsp fish sauce
2 tsp smoked paprika
2 tsp garlic powder
2 lbs head-on prawns,
    shells and tails on

Glaze

½ cup dried hibiscus
    flowers
1 cup granulated sugar
2 Tbsp fish sauce
2 Tbsp red wine vinegar
3 strips lemon peel
One 4 in piece ginger,
    peeled and finely
    grated

Citrus Salad

3 oranges
1 grapefruit
1 lime
¼ red onion, cut into
    thin half moons
3 Tbsp chopped
    cilantro stems
1 Tbsp hand-crushed
    pink peppercorns
1 tsp extra-virgin olive oil
1 tsp Fragrant Chile Oil
    (page 38)
Kosher salt

Crispy Garlic Chips (page
    37), for serving

These head-on prawns can take the edge right out of a gloomy winter day. The glaze, made from dried hibiscus flowers, offers a natural acidity that's amplified when reduced, alongside red wine vinegar. When drizzled over the prawns, umami-rich from the fish sauce marinade, and eaten with the citrus salad and crispy garlic chips, this dish brings your body directly to a warm island paradise. Consider making the glaze and garlic chips in advance.

TO MAKE THE SHRIMP: In a large bowl, combine the fish sauce, paprika, and garlic powder. Add the shrimp and gently toss to coat. Let marinate in the refrigerator for 1 hour before grilling.

TO MAKE THE GLAZE: In a medium saucepan, bring the hibiscus flowers and 2 cups of water to a boil over medium heat. Turn the heat to medium and simmer until bright pink in color and infused with a hibiscus flavor, about 5 minutes. Pour through a fine-mesh sieve into a bowl; discard any solids. Return the pink liquid to the pot, add the sugar, fish sauce, vinegar, and lemon peel and bring to a boil over high heat. Turn the heat to low and simmer until thickened to a syrup-like consistency, 15 to 20 minutes. Pour through a fine-mesh sieve into a bowl; discard any solids. Set aside to cool then add the ginger.

TO MAKE THE CITRUS SALAD: Use a paring knife to cut the ends off the oranges, grapefruit, and lime to give each one a stable base. Remove the peels from the flesh and cut the flesh into ½ in thick rounds; discard the peels or reserve for another use. In a medium bowl, toss the orange, grapefruit, and lime rounds with the red onion, cilantro stems, and pink peppercorns. Set aside.

Heat a grill to 400 to 450°F. Alternatively, place a cast-iron skillet over medium-high heat until searing hot. Working in batches as needed, add the prawns and quickly grill or sear until the shells are crispy and the shrimp is cooked through, 1 to 2 minutes per side.

TO SERVE: Drizzle the citrus salad with olive oil and chile oil, season with salt, toss to combine, and plate on a large serving dish. Arrange the prawns on top and drizzle with the hibiscus glaze. Top off with a dash of chile oil and sprinkle liberally with crispy fried garlic.

SCALLOP AND JALAPEÑO SKEWERS WITH SEAWEED AND SESAME SALSA

Serves 4 to 6

Seaweed and Sesame Salsa

½ cup dried hijiki

4 sheets dried nori

5 anchovy fillets, chopped

1 cup lacto-fermented greens, such as mustard, turnip, or radish (see Lacto-Fermented Carrots, page 43, or purchase at your local Asian specialty store), chopped

½ cup toasted sesame seeds

1 cup rice vinegar

¼ cup extra-virgin olive oil

1 Tbsp toasted sesame oil

Scallop and Jalapeño Skewers

10 in wooden or metal skewers

1½ lbs fresh sea scallops

4 to 6 jalapeños, seeded and cut into 1 in chunks

1 red onion, cut in ¼ in thick half moons

1 pt cherry tomatoes, cut in half

Kosher salt

Neutral oil, for grilling

We created this dish for our outdoor pandemic project, Fuego 69, and it skyrocketed to the top of our most-ordered menu items. The umami from the seaweed blends deliciously with the fermented greens that meld perfectly with the heat of the jalapeño and sweet scallops. These skewers are a great addition to summer barbeques and are best seared on a cast-iron plancha over a wood-fired grill. Alternatively, if cooking on the stove, just make sure your pan is super-duper hot, so the heat will char the outside of the scallops, creating a crust-like texture, while retaining a sweet, moist center. If using wooden or bamboo skewers, soak them for an hour in warm water to prevent burning.

TO MAKE THE SEAWEED AND SESAME SALSA: Bring 2 cups of water to a boil. Put the dried hijiki in a medium bowl, add the hot water, and let stand for 10 minutes. Drain well; discard the liquid and set the hijiki aside.

Meanwhile, heat a cast-iron skillet over medium-high heat. Add the nori and gently toast, flipping as needed, until it crisps up and bubbles, 1 to 2 minutes per side. Transfer to a food processor and grind into a fine powder. Remove from the food processor and set aside.

Put the anchovies in the food processor and pulse to a paste. Add the hijiki, lacto-fermented greens, and sesame seeds and gently pulse to coarsely chop and combine. Transfer to a large bowl. Add the rice vinegar, olive oil, and sesame oil and stir to combine and loosen the mixture. Sprinkle in the nori powder and stir to combine. Season with salt and set aside.

TO MAKE THE SCALLOP AND JALAPEÑO SKEWERS: Use your fingers to remove the "foot" from each scallop. If the scallops are large, cut them in half widthwise. Pat dry with paper towels. Build each skewer, alternating between scallops, jalapeño, red onion, and tomato until the skewer is full. Season generously with salt.

Heat a grill to high heat. Alternatively, place a cast-iron skillet over high heat until searing hot. Brush the skewers with neutral oil to prevent sticking and then add to the grill or skillet and sear until the scallops are deeply browned and can be easily removed from the grill or skillet, 1 to 2 minutes. Flip and sear the other side until deeply browned, about 1 minute.

TO SERVE: Arrange the skewers on plates and spoon the seaweed and sesame salsa on top.

SCALLOPS A LA DIOSA

Serves 2 to 4

Guava Sauce

2 cups frozen guava purée
3 garlic cloves, peeled
and smashed
1 shallot, peeled and
quartered
1 fresh Fresno chile, cut
into 3 or 4 pieces
Kosher salt
2 Tbsp unsalted butter

Meyer Lemon Garnish

1 Meyer lemon

Olive Coulis

1 cup oil-cured black
olives, pitted
⅔ cup olive oil

Scallops

1½ lbs fresh sea scallops
1 Tbsp kosher salt
1 Tbsp canola oil

Sexy, romantic, and a little bit dangerous, these scallops deliver an unexpected combination of flavors that work surprisingly well together. Think of it as a kinky marinara sauce. Diosa means "goddess" in Spanish, and we thought it an apt name for a sauce made from sweet guava pulp and seasoned with the warm heat of Fresno chiles. Guava has a very high pectin content, which means it will begin to set and hold its shape when it cools. Be prepared to serve it immediately or coax it back to life by warming it over low heat. Serve with a side of buttered toast.

TO MAKE THE GUAVA SAUCE: In a blender, combine the guava purée, garlic, and shallot and blend until smooth. Gradually add the chile, blending until smooth and adding more as needed for additional heat. Pour through a fine-mesh sieve into a medium saucepan. Season with salt and set aside.

TO MAKE THE MEYER LEMON GARNISH: Use a peeler to remove long strips of peel from the lemon. Reserve the lemon for the olive coulis. Use a knife to remove any pith from the lemon peels. Stack the peels and slice them into long, thin strips. Set aside.

TO MAKE THE OLIVE COULIS: Juice the reserved lemon and put the juice in a blender. Add the olives and blend until smooth. With the blender on, gradually add the olive oil, blending to emulsify.

TO MAKE THE SCALLOPS: Remove the foot from the scallops, pat dry with paper towels, and season with salt. In a large skillet over medium-high heat, heat the canola oil until nearly smoking. Working in batches as needed, carefully add the scallops flat side down and sear until golden brown on the bottom, 1 to 2 minutes. Flip and sear until the other side is golden brown, about 1 more minute. Immediately remove from the pan and keep warm while you cook the remaining scallops.

TO SERVE: Warm the guava sauce, add the butter, and stir to melt. Pour the warm guava sauce on a platter and arrange the scallops on top. Use a small spoon to top the scallops with the olive coulis. Garnish with Meyer lemon and eat, eat, eat!

Categories Are Annoying and Some Wines Defy Them

Like rosatos, ramatos are Italian in origin and another type of skin-contact wine. Ramato translates to something close to "copper" or "auburn" in English and is made using a centuries-old process that involves macerating pinot grigio grapes on their skins for a prolonged period of time. Pinot grigio grapes have skins that are a unique silvery pink color that produces wines that are a gorgeous warm dusty pink. Some consider it a rosé alternative, others see it as a "new" area of orange wine. Why does this gorgeous pink drink have to live in the context of its more established relatives? A ramato has enough of everything for everyone and can satisfy many different drinkers at the same time. It could be a new way to keep the wine peace between your rosé friends, your orange wine friends, your red wine friends, and your friends who want a dry white but will settle for anything dry. This style of wine provides enough of an adventure for those who want to explore and enough structure for those who want it—a true non-binary icon.

PAN-FRIED SARDINES

Serves 2 to 4

Schmear

2 garlic heads, halved
    horizontally
Extra-virgin olive oil
Kosher salt
1 fresh Fresno chile,
    cut into thin strips
Zest of 1 lemon

Salsa

2 tomatillos, finely diced
1 small baby fennel bulb,
    shaved, fronds reserved
½ red onion, finely diced
½ cup freshly squeezed
    lime juice (from
    3 to 4 large limes)
2 Tbsp chopped
    flat-leaf parsley
1 Tbsp oregano leaves
1 Tbsp pine nuts, toasted
2 tsp kosher salt
¼ cup extra-virgin olive oil

Sardines

6 to 10 medium sardines,
    cleaned and gutted
Kosher salt
Neutral oil
1 lime, quartered

Sardines are full of nutrient-rich deliciousness that we love to indulge in whenever their season hits our part of the world. Ask your fishmonger for details on when to find these tasty little fish in your area. Here, we pair them with a fresh tomatillo salad and a schmear of roasted garlic. If you *think* that you don't love sardines, we're committed to changing your mind. Feel free to make the schmear and salsa a day ahead for an easy and quick dinner the following night.

TO MAKE THE SCHMEAR: Preheat the oven to 400°F. Drizzle olive oil over the garlic and sprinkle with a pinch of salt. Wrap each halved garlic head individually in aluminum foil and roast until soft and golden brown, about 45 minutes. Set aside to cool. Squeeze the garlic from its skin. Season with salt, fold in Fresno chile and lemon zest, and set aside. Store for up to 1 week in the refrigerator.

WHILE THE GARLIC IS ROASTING, MAKE THE SALSA: In a small bowl, combine the tomatillos, shaved fennel, red onion, lime juice, parsley, oregano, pine nuts, and salt. Let stand to marinate for about 20 minutes. Drizzle in the olive oil, stirring to incorporate. Set aside. It lasts 2 to 3 days in the refrigerator.

TO MAKE THE SARDINES: Pat the sardines dry with paper towels. With a sharp knife, score the flesh, making 3 even strokes on each side. Generously season with salt. Heat 1 tablespoon of the neutral oil in a large frying pan over high heat until piping hot. Add the sardines and cook, flipping once, until the skin is crisp and golden and the flesh easily pulls off the bone, about 3 minutes per side.

TO SERVE: Spread the schmear on a serving platter. Arrange the sardines on top and squeeze the lime over the fish. Spoon tomatillo salsa over the sardines and garnish with the delicate fennel fronds strewn about.

WHOLE FRIED FISH

Serves 1 to 2

Vinaigrette

4 garlic cloves, chopped
One 2 in piece ginger,
  peeled and chopped
3 Tbsp fish sauce, plus
  more as needed
2 Tbsp freshly squeezed
  orange juice
2 Tbsp freshly squeezed
  lime juice, plus more
  as needed
1 cup canola oil

Fish

2 qts neutral oil, for frying
1 whole fish (ask your
  fishmonger to gut
  and scale)
1 cup Frying Flour
  (page 46)
1 large handful pea shoots
  or any tender green,
  such as tatsoi or
  mustard greens,
  for serving
Cilantro, mint, and dill,
  for serving

Where would we be without this dish? Somewhere sad and lonely, that's where we'd be! Whole fried fish is by far our most popular dish at the restaurant. We took notes from the way Carla's Ecuadorian aunties would fry fish in their paila, a huge brass cauldron. The addition of pea shoots and herbs, as well as our vinaigrette, was inspired by the whole fish served in many Vietnamese restaurants that's often delightfully smothered with ginger. We love to use branzino, black sea bass, and porgy, but you should use what is local and in season. At Lil' Deb's Oasis, when the fish is brought to the table, we explain that the preferred way to eat this fish is to pour the sauce over the top and then just go at it with your fingers. Eating this dish with a fork feels wrong, so don't do it!

TO MAKE THE VINAIGRETTE: In a blender, combine the garlic, ginger, fish sauce, orange juice, and lime juice and blend until fully combined. With the blender on, gradually add the canola oil, blending to fully emulsify, about 2 minutes. Taste and season as needed with fish sauce and lime juice until gingery and bright with deep umami undertones. Store for up to 1 week in the refrigerator.

TO MAKE THE FISH: In a large heavy-bottomed pot over medium-high heat, heat the neutral oil to 350°F on a deep-fry thermometer (see frying guidelines, page 45). Line a baking sheet with paper towels and set near the stove or a deep fryer.

Pat the fish dry with paper towels. With a sharp knife, score the flesh, making 3 even strokes on each side and leaving 1 in spaces between each slit. Coat the fish in the fry flour, including under its fins and inside the cavity.

When the oil reaches 350°F, carefully add the fish and fry, turning with tongs or a slotted spoon, until golden brown all over, about 4 minutes per side. Use a knife to check for doneness, making sure the flesh is no longer translucent and easily lifts away from the bone. Transfer to the paper towel–lined baking sheet.

TO SERVE: Create a bed of pea shoots and herbs on a platter and arrange the fish on top. Pour vinaigrette all over the fish or serve it on the side if you prefer to dunk. Please, please use your fingers, lifting segments of fried fish, dipping and eating, dipping and eating. Delight, laugh, and don't forget to lick your fingers.

LOBSTER RIVER DINNER

Serves 10 to 15

Mustardy, Gingery Tomato Sauce
Makes 4 cups

¼ cup extra-virgin olive oil
4 garlic cloves
One 15 oz can tomato
    purée
2 Tbsp kosher salt, plus
    more to taste
½ cup Pickled Mustard
    Seeds (page 44)
Two 1 in pieces peeled
    ginger, julienned
¼ cup apple cider vinegar
1 Tbsp freshly ground
    black pepper

Lovage Aioli
Makes 4 cups

Lovage is only available
in season either from
a farmers' market or a
specialty grocery store.
But don't pull your hair out
trying to find it—celery
leaves, parsley, and mint
make great substitutes.

1 cup neutral oil
1 cup extra-virgin olive oil
2 packed cups lovage
    leaves or celery leaves,
    parsley, or mint
8 small garlic cloves
Zest of 1 lemon
4 Tbsp freshly squeezed
    lemon juice (from
    about 2 lemons)
4 tsp kosher salt
4 large egg yolks
6 tsp ice water

The key to a party that feels truly spontaneous is not a sexy secret, it's practical. It involves knowing what kind of party you want to throw and a ton of planning. While we trust you can pull together a fantastic last-minute fête, we recommend gathering your ingredients and materials a day or two in advance, so the day of your party can truly feel effortless and fun.

While dinner can be designed around a lot of little dishes that are eaten together, it can also be one big showstopper like lobster. And a really memorable meal can lead to the creation of a new annual holiday, with friends saying, "Let's do this again next year!" Most important is not to stress. As the host, you set the vibe. Dinner guests, like sharks and middle schoolers, can sense when their host is not having a good time.

If you don't live near a body of water, don't worry—you can throw this party anywhere. We happen to live near the Hudson River and often take advantage of its long shoreline. You can also throw this party in a park, or your own backyard. Just pick a location that feels right for you.

If finding a river isn't an obstacle enough, lobsters are expensive! We recommend throwing this party only when lobsters are in season, or your party's price tag will go up. You can choose to serve crab, crawdaddies, or shrimp. Honestly, you could serve just grilled vegetables and the sauce recipes will bring them to full, robust life. We also believe that the host doesn't have to pay for everything. Consider asking your invitees to contribute to the cost of the meal. We promise it's not tacky. It's a cool way of mutually supporting each other to have fun together without breaking anyone's bank.

Our last hot tip for a sensual and abundant group dinner al fresco is to ask a friend to be your designated alcohol distributor. That way, you'll have a buddy to help ensure that bottles are being opened and everyone's voracious thirst (including yours) is being quenched, while you're busy making memories in your outdoor kitchen.

TO MAKE THE MUSTARDY, GINGERY TOMATO SAUCE: In a medium saucepan over low heat, warm the olive oil until glistening. Add the garlic and slowly cook, stirring, until soft and fragrant without taking on too much color (do not caramelize or brown), about 5 minutes. Add the tomato purée and 1 cup of water and bring to a boil. Turn the heat to low and simmer until the garlic flavor has infused with the tomatoes, about 10 minutes. Season with 2 tablespoons salt. Turn off the heat. In a medium bowl, combine the mustard seeds, ginger, apple cider vinegar, and black pepper. Add the tomato sauce and stir to combine. Season with salt to taste. Transfer to an airtight container and refrigerate overnight until ready to use.

Grilled Vegetables

Japanese eggplants,
summer squash,
zucchini, broccoli
rabe, or other seasonal
summer vegetables (we
recommend 1 Japanese
eggplant, half a squash,
and a few stalks of
broccoli rabe per guest)

Lobster

1 lobster per person
(in season and alive,
kept very cold)
Kosher salt
Squeeze bottle full
of neutral oil for
easy transport and
application

Party supplies for dining al fresco

Here's a list of items you
need to have on hand,
and some items you don't
need but might want to
have around:

**MUST-HAVES IN NO
PARTICULAR ORDER:**
Tongs—the longer
the better
Kitchen towels
Cutting board
Cleaver for butchering
lobsters
Bowls for sauces
Extra salt and oil
Hammers or nutcrackers
for the lobster claws
2 bundles of firewood
(don't forget kindling!)
Matches or a stick lighter
Metal grate (a home oven
rack or grill grate)
Garbage bags to bring
your trash home with
you—leave no trace!
Reusable containers for
prepped vegetables

TO MAKE THE LOVAGE AIOLI: In a spouted measuring cup, whisk together the canola oil and olive oil. In a food processor, combine the lovage, garlic, lemon zest and juice, and salt and pulse until smooth. Add the egg yolks and pulse until fully incorporated. With the food processor on, gradually add half of the oil mixture, blending until emulsified, about 2 minutes. Drizzle in the ice water, followed by the remaining oil mixture. Season with salt as needed—the aioli should be fresh and bright in flavor, smooth and rich in texture, and light green in color. Transfer to an airtight container and refrigerate until ready to use or for up to 1 week—slather over everything for the rest of your life.

TO PREP THE GRILLED VEGETABLES: Wash and prep the veggies before heading to your party zone. Larger vegetables, like zucchini or summer squash, should be cut into smaller pieces at home. Leave smaller vegetables whole, as they'll char nicely over the wood fire. Japanese eggplant is the perfect size for grilling whole, which means less prep for you! Store them in airtight containers or bags to take to the party zone.

TO PREP THE LOBSTER: Be brave! We're here to do our best hand-holding. We love you! You can do this, and once you've done it, you'll feel more confident working with seafood in the kitchen.

Butchering a lobster can be intimidating. You are, after all, taking a life. We recommend finding your center before beginning and saying sweet gentle words of appreciation to the lobsters as you move through this process. One helpful tip is that the colder you keep the lobsters, the calmer they will be, as colder temperatures slow down their metabolism, making it easier and safer for you to handle. Keep lobsters cold (but not on ice). Butcher them as close to grilling time as possible.

HOW TO BUTCHER A LIVE LOBSTER:
1. Place a large cutting board on top of a moistened kitchen towel to keep your board in place while you work.
2. Make sure your favorite cleaver is sharp and have dry towels on hand.
3. Place the lobster on your cutting board, belly side up (rubber bands on its claws). We like to place one hand on its belly and say nice things to it, perhaps thanking it for its life. This helps to calm both you and the lobster.
4. Place the cleaver sharp side down and lengthwise on the center of the lobster's belly. Keeping one hand on the handle, use the other hand to apply pressure to the top of the cleaver, firmly rocking back and forth.
5. Getting through the belly of the lobster is fairly easy, as it is more tender than its outer shell, so you'll have to place additional pressure on the cleaver when you hit the opposite side of the lobster. Do this by placing the flat of your hand on the top of your cleaver and pressing down with your body weight.
6. Make sure to cut through the head and tail to split the lobster in half lengthwise. You'll have to lift and move the cleaver to the exact location you need to cut through. Wipe down your cleaver with a kitchen towel between movements, to prevent slippage.

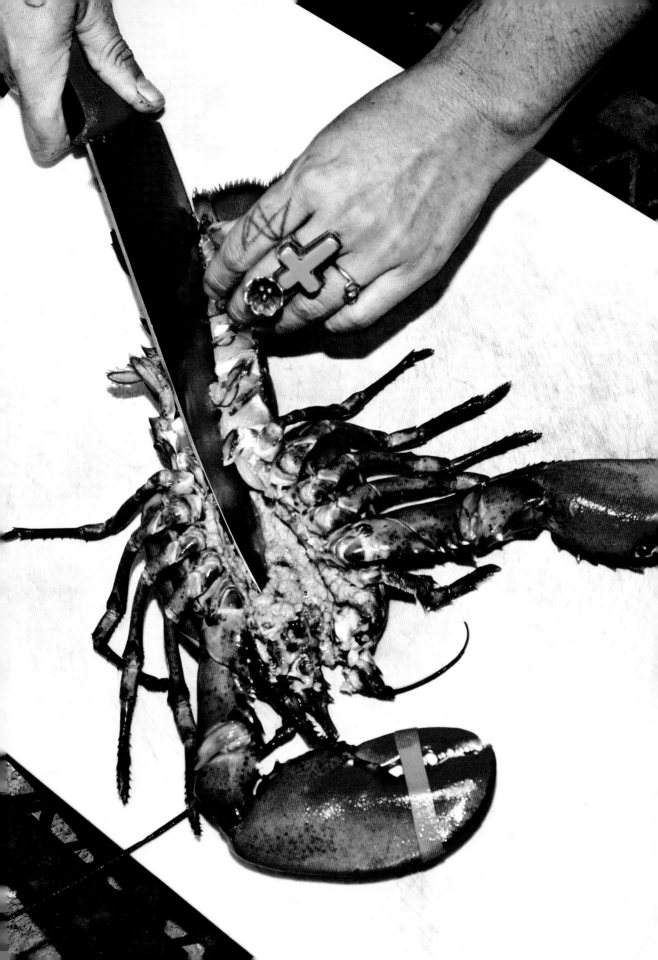

Bucket for transporting your lobsters

Old newspapers, aka your tablecloth (no need for plates!)

Cold wine or beer (If you find a suitable babbling brook, put your bottles directly in the waterflow to keep them cool—just make sure they don't get carried away with the current!)

Wine opener

Cups for cold wine or beer

NICE TO HAVE ON HAND, BUT NOT NECESSARY:

Cinder block "table legs" (reuse for an outdoor planter!)

Plywood "tabletop"

Candles or lamps for after sunset

Tarps or blankets

Cloth napkins (please don't use paper)

Plates and spoons

Cooler with ice

Name cards (because no one will expect you to have them at a picnic)

7. Remove and discard the digestive tract and egg sack.

8. If not grilling immediately, refrigerate lobster pieces in an airtight bag or container. If transporting to your party zone immediately, place them into a bucket or cooler with ice.

Party Day

On the day of your party, rise and shine after a good night's sleep. Have your coffee or tea and make sure to eat a nice breakfast. Take a minute to care for yourself—give yourself love in order to give love to others. While you sip your tea, make a checklist for everything you need to bring with you. (Don't forget the wine opener!) Start to pack things up, ideally in an organized way—for example, all your foodstuff in one box, all your fire equipment in another, all the table settings somewhere else. Load everything into your chosen mode of transport, check your list again, and head to your party zone. You'll want to arrive about 1 to 2 hours before everyone else, so you can set up, be prepared to make some creative decisions, and get settled in peace.

When you arrive at your party zone, it's time to set yourself up for success. Place each of your boxes in their zones (fire, food prep, table zone). Now you can begin to haul rocks for your fire, gather firewood if you didn't buy any, and set up your outdoor kitchen. Have your designated party-day friend set the table and chill the wine, either in the river or on ice.

HOW TO MAKE A FIRE: Don't forget to practice fire safety when you make a fire without a grill box. Use rocks to build a circle for your fire or build it close to the water (be aware of whether the tide is low or high). You ideally want your dining area to be close to the fire, so you aren't doing too much running back and forth.

Making a fire takes patience, practice, and a lot of dry wood. It also takes kindling. Purchase it with your firewood bundles or gather dry twigs, sticks, leaves, or even dry pine needles. We don't recommend using a fire starter as the noxious fumes will impart chemical flavors into your food.

1. Gather rocks and stones to create a small circle around your campfire. Alternatively, use cinder blocks to create a box-like structure to contain your fire. Build the circle or box high enough to place the grill grate over the top, leaving 3 or 4 in of space between the fire and grill.

2. In the center of your circle, build a small pile, pyramid style, with kindling. This will be the nexus source of heat that you'll build your larger fire around. You can also use crumpled up newspaper to help jump-start your flame. Think about space and airflow, because a fire needs some room to breathe. Just like in a relationship, a smothered fire can't maintain heat—keep that in mind for your personal life, too!

3. Using medium-size logs, build a triangle around your kindling pile, slightly overlapping the ends of the logs over each other to create space for air to move around. The triangle should get tighter closer to the top without disturbing your kindling. Use 3 to 5 logs for this step, reserving the biggest logs for later.

4. Light your kindling using matches or a lighter.

5. Watch the fire. Ideally, the kindling should begin to ignite the logs. If necessary, add a crossbeam over the top of the triangle to encourage the kindling to carry heat over to the rest of the wood.

6. Place the grill grate over the fire and allow it to heat up. Do a little heat test. You'll know it's ready for grilling when you hold your hand about a foot above the fire and you want to quickly move it away.

Grilling Time

TO CHAR THE VEGETABLES: Lightly dress them with oil and salt then put them directly on the grill grate and char, turning frequently with your handy tong, until fork-tender, 5 to 10 minutes, depending on the vegetables you've selected. Transfer to a tray and keep warm.

TO MAKE THE LOBSTER CENTERPIECE: Make sure the grill is very hot. Season the lobsters with salt then put the halves, shell side down, directly on the grill grate and grill, flipping as needed, until the meat loses its translucency and turns white and firm, 3 to 4 minutes per side. As you keep grilling, arrange cooked lobsters across the table. Think about sculptures, Viking gatherings, fairy feasts. And don't forget to save at least one piece of lobster for yourself!

At this point, your table is set, the wine is flowing, your friends are hungry. Distribute hammers/nutcrackers, alongside your freshly grilled lobsters, on your makeshift table. Dip lobster pieces into the aioli and mustardy, gingery tomato sauce. Feed bites to your friends. Kiss your lover. And if you have the forethought to be that girl, save and freeze the shells for making stock or lobster bisque.

Don't forget to clean up and leave no trace. Simply roll up the newsprint with all the food scraps caught inside and toss into that trash bag you brought with you. We love a magic moment when the work does itself.

Say goodnight to your guests (unless there's an after-party) and bask in the glory of a dinner well thrown.

How Much Wine Do I Need for My Party?

All guests and their respective thirst levels are different, but our recommendations land in the range of making sure everyone has one to three glasses of wine each. We suggest two bottles for every three guests. We tend to follow a 1:1 ratio for our own parties due to our commitment to hedonism, but 2:3 works for a sensible fête. Our biggest tip, however, is that a little hoarding goes a long way. If you, like us, tend to drink more than three glasses of wine at a party and have six guests, put four bottles in the fridge and squirrel away two extra bottles, which will save you later on when your guests say, "I wish we had just one more bottle!" And last, but not least, make sure your guests are able to get home safely. Have a taxi service number or rideshare app on hand or a designated driver. Fun is fun but keeping your friends safe is more important!

CHAPTER SIX

PILLOW TALK

SWEET INDULGENCES TO FULLY SATISFY

RECIPES

Every book needs its final chapter, every story its end. A good meal must have the same—a little something to extend the night…just a little bit longer. A good dessert can be simply "a little something sweet" or a celebratory occasion, and we LOVE celebratory occasions. A good dessert is like a kiss goodbye: It can be anything from a satisfying, quick little moment to a passionate, drawn-out affair. These recipes will bring a little sweetness to the end of your night (or the middle of your day), so come with us and step into a world of indulgence and pleasure.

ABUELA'S FLAN

Serves 8 to 12

Spiced Milk

2 Tbsp cardamom pods
2 Tbsp coriander seeds
2 Tbsp black peppercorns
1 Tbsp whole allspice
    berries
1 cinnamon stick
1 Tbsp fennel seeds
2½ cups heavy cream
2½ cups whole milk
Peel of 1 lemon, pith
    removed
Peel of 1 orange, pith
    removed
1 tsp kosher salt

Caramel

1½ cups granulated sugar

Egg Custard Base

6 large eggs
6 large egg yolks
1¼ cups granulated sugar
1 tsp vanilla bean paste

"Grandma knows best," goes the adage. And we agree, don't you? We love this smooth, rich custard, with its background of warm spices, that's served cold at the end of a long meal. And as Carla's grandmother always says, the secret to the perfect flan is trusting that it's finished. Flan will always have a healthy jiggle, even fully cooked, so trust the process, or you'll risk overcooking it and making a sweet egg scramble instead. And as Grandma also says, "safety first!"—please use extreme caution when preparing the caramel.

Set a rack in the middle of the oven and preheat the oven to 350°F.

TO MAKE THE SPICED MILK: In a large pot over medium heat, toast the cardamom, coriander, peppercorns, allspice, cinnamon, and fennel seeds until fragrant, about 2 minutes. Add the heavy cream, milk, lemon peel, orange peel, and salt and slowly warm over medium-low heat until hot but not boiling. Turn off the heat, cover, and let steep for 20 minutes. Pour through a fine-mesh sieve into a bowl and let stand. Cool to lukewarm; discard any solids.

The next step might feel challenging, but you'll get the hang of it. Mostly, it takes patience and careful observation. Don't disturb the sugar too much as it melts—hold back from stirring it excessively. At the same time, you don't want the bottom layer of sugar to burn, so notice when it has reached the melting point, and begin stirring before it starts to smoke. Read that sentence again, take a deep breath, and trust yourself! Be careful: overmixing will lead to crystallization, which is when the sugar hardens beyond repair and refuses to melt down again. Keep this delicate balance in mind as you work. Here we go!

TO MAKE THE CARAMEL: Put the sugar in a large nonstick pan over medium-low heat. Watching very carefully, let the sugar cook until the bottom layer starts to soften. Using a heat-resistant rubber spatula, stir the sugar just enough to move it around and expose a new layer to the bottom of the hot pan. Continue cooking, without stirring, and watch for the bottom layer to soften again. Again, use the spatula to stir the sugar just enough to move it around and expose a new layer to the bottom of the pan. Repeat this process once or twice more until all the sugar has melted. Continue cooking the sugar over medium-low heat, watching carefully, until the sugar starts to caramelize—bubbles will appear, and the color will turn golden brown. At this point, the sugar can burn quickly. As soon as it turns a deep, rich brown, immediately and carefully pour it into a 2 in deep 9 in round cake pan, carefully turning the pan to spread the caramel evenly on the bottom. Again, be careful—the caramel is extremely hot! Wear oven mitts when handling the hot nonstick pan and the cake pan after you pour in the caramel—it will heat up very fast.

Set aside to cool completely.

TO MAKE THE EGG CUSTARD BASE: In a large bowl, vigorously whisk together the eggs, egg yolks, sugar, and vanilla until the eggs are fully incorporated into the sugar. Gradually add the cooled milk mixture, whisking until fully incorporated. Pour through a fine-mesh sieve into a bowl and set aside; discard any solids. Strain again and discard any clumpy bits. (Don't skip this step, as it will ensure your flan is smooth and creamy.)

Put the caramel-filled pan in a 3 in deep baking dish. Pour 1 to 2 inches of boiling water into the baking dish without splashing any into the cake pan. Pour the flan mixture over the caramel in the pan, leaving ¼ in of space at the top. Cover the baking dish with aluminum foil, sealing it well. Gently place the baking dish in the center of the oven and bake for 40 to 45 minutes. Test the flan by inserting a toothpick into the center. If it comes out wet or streaky, bake for 5 more minutes. Be careful not to overbake the flan, as the eggs will begin to "scramble" around the edges. When ready, the flan should move as a single unit when you gently shake the pan. Flan will be wiggly, and some condensation will collect at the top as it steams, so don't let the moisture fool you. Total cook time depends on the accuracy of your oven temperature, so trust the jiggle more than the time!

Carefully remove the flan pan from the water bath, set on a rack, and let cool completely, about 1 hour. Refrigerate for at least 2 hours or overnight.

TO SERVE: Run a knife or offset spatula around the edge of the pan. Place a serving platter with a lip (to catch caramel juice) on top of the pan. Placing one hand on the platter, and the other under the pan, bravely flip them in a single motion, ending with the platter on the bottom and the pan on top. Carefully lift the pan up to reveal the glossy, mirrored surface of your flan. Serve cold, in sexy slices, or simply eat it with a spoon.

Birthday Celebration (Why We Sing)

At the restaurant, when a dessert order comes in with the note "birthday," our staff prepares for the performance. It all started when a former employee and dear friend came for dinner to celebrate his birthday. We wanted to smother him with an embarrassing amount of love. Using the resources we had on hand, we made aluminum foil hats for the staff and a giant foil tiara for the birthday boy. When the moment arrived, we donned our hats and began a processional out from the kitchen. With the flan ablaze, we sang "Happy Birthday," while banging on pots and other makeshift instruments and crowned our friend the king of the eve. At that moment the whole restaurant felt synergetic. Everyone, staff and customers, sang at the top of their lungs, all inhibitions out the door. We try to recreate that moment whenever we get a birthday ticket in and encourage you to celebrate with the same improvisational gusto.

BANANA LOCA

Serves 2 to 4

Dulce de Leche

One 14 oz can sweetened
    condensed milk

Fried Bananas

1 cup rice flour
½ cup white sesame seeds,
    plus more for garnish
¼ cup tapioca starch
2 Tbsp granulated sugar
½ Tbsp kosher salt
One 12 oz can cold seltzer
2 cups neutral oil
2 ripe bananas, peeled
Vanilla ice cream

Nothing beats a banana split, and this sexy, indulgent recipe—crispy, creamy, hot, and cold—takes it to the next level. We fry our bananas, Burmese style in a batter made from gluten-free tapioca and rice flours and sesame seeds, and we make our own dulce de leche. We recommend making this dessert for yourself or a love interest you want to impress. Nothing hits the spot, or the heart, like a homemade dessert.

TO MAKE THE DULCE DE LECHE: The instructions for this scrumptious, melt-in-your-mouth treat are on page 192.

TO FRY THE BANANAS: In a medium-size bowl, combine the rice flour, sesame seeds, tapioca starch, sugar, and salt and whisk thoroughly to fully combine. Set aside

In a medium-size heavy-bottomed pot over medium-high heat, bring 2 cups of oil to 350°F on a candy or deep-fat thermometer (see frying guidelines, page 45). Line a baking sheet with paper towels and set near the stove.

Meanwhile, gradually add the seltzer to the flour mix—you may only need about half of the can—stirring until a thick batter forms (think pancake batter). Don't worry about the lumps.

When the oil reaches 350°F, peel and dredge each banana in the sesame seed batter. Working in batches as needed, carefully add the banana to the oil and fry, using tongs or a slotted spoon to gently move the banana around, until the batter is a golden, light brown color. Transfer to the paper towel–lined baking sheet and season with salt.

TO SERVE: Place the fried banana in a bowl. Serve hot with a scoop of vanilla ice cream. Drizzle dulce de leche over it and finish with a sprinkle of sesame seeds.

COCONUT SNOW

Serves 4

Two 12 oz cans
    unsweetened full-fat
    coconut milk
Zest and juice of 6 to 8
    limes, depending on
    your sour tooth
¼ to ½ cup simple syrup
    (see page 52),
    depending on your
    sweet tooth
2 to 4 Tbsp rum or cachaça,
    depending on your
    booze tooth
¼ cup chopped toasted
    pistachios, for serving
Fancy flaky salt, such as
    Maldon or black
    sea salt, for serving

Cool down on a hot summer's eve with this refreshing dessert. It's a crowd pleaser. We took it off of the menu, only to reinstate it after requests from customers, who longed for this creamy yet airy dessert. At Lil' Deb's, we serve it sans booze, but the version here calls for alcohol, because it's more fun and it helps keep the snow from turning into a block of ice.

In a 2 quart cake pan, loaf pan, or metal bowl, whisk together the coconut milk, lime zest and juice, simple syrup, and rum. Cover tightly with plastic wrap and freeze until completely frozen, at least 4 hours or overnight.

TO SERVE: Use a fork to scrape the coconut mixture and create a light, snowy texture. Spoon the snow into small bowls and sprinkle with the pistachios and your fanciest salt.

STRAWBERRY ROSE BATIDO

Serves 2 to 4

4 cups frozen strawberries
1 to 2 cups whole milk
1 to 2 Tbsp rose water
1 tsp pure vanilla extract
    or 1 vanilla bean
Pinch of kosher salt

Romance yourself and/or your crush with this taste-of-summer milkshake. If you happen to crave this recipe during strawberry season, take advantage of those tender-sweet fresh berries and simply add a cup of ice.

In a blender, combine the strawberries, milk, rose water, and vanilla, adding more or less milk to create a thinner or thicker shake and more or less rose water to suit your taste. Blend on high until smooth. Season with salt. Divide into glasses and enjoy immediately :)

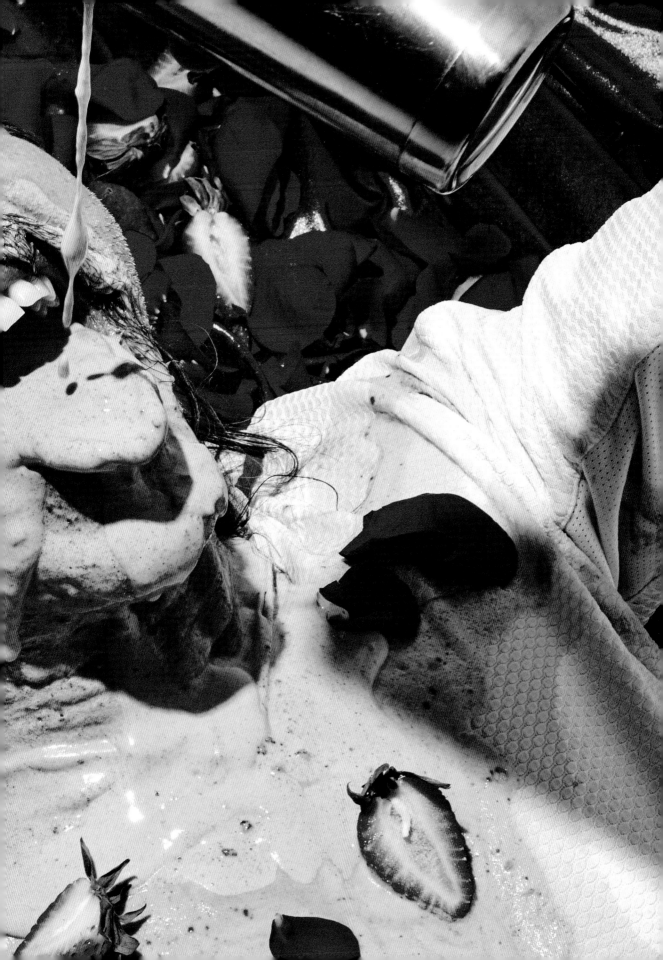

PICARONES

Serves 4 to 6

Pineapple Syrup

½ pineapple

1½ cups palm or
    coconut sugar

1 Tbsp lime zest

1 in piece ginger,
    peeled and grated

Picarones

5 cardamom pods

2 cinnamon sticks

One 1 in piece fresh ginger,
    peel and chopped

2 tsp coriander seeds

2 tsp black peppercorns

1 tsp cloves

1 tsp allspice berries

1 tsp fennel seeds

1 lb sweet potatoes
    or Japanese yams,
    peeled and cubed

1⅓ cups whole milk

2 large eggs, beaten

3 Tbsp granulated sugar

1 tsp ground ginger

¼ tsp Magic Dust (page 35),
    plus more for serving

2 cups all-purpose flour

1½ tsp baking powder

Pinch of kosher salt

2 qts neutral oil, for frying

½ cup powdered sugar,
    to garnish

These crispy, sweet potato fritters hail from Peru, where they are traditionally formed into a donut shape. Indigenous people originally made them without the use of gluten, utilizing only pumpkin and sweet potato. Wheat was later introduced to the recipe, via colonization by Spanish forces, and the modern-day recipe includes all three ingredients. Our recipe omits the pumpkin, because we prefer the natural sweetness of sweet potato. We recommend making the syrup a day ahead. And please use the leftover pineapple to make our Pineapple Ambrosia (page 119)!

TO MAKE THE PINEAPPLE SYRUP: Peel the pineapple and reserve the flesh for another use. Cut the skins into 2 in wide strips. Put a medium saucepan over high heat until smoking hot. Put the pineapple skin, flesh side down, in the pan and char until almost burnt, 2 to 3 minutes. Turn the heat to low and let the pan cool slightly. Add the sugar and 1 cup of water, turn the heat to medium-low, and cook until the liquid is syrupy and runs thickly off a spoon, about 20 minutes. Strain and discard the pineapple skins. Add the lime zest and ginger and stir to incorporate. Set aside until ready to use or store in an airtight container in the refrigerator for up to a month.

TO MAKE THE PICARONES: Wrap the cardamom, cinnamon sticks, ginger, coriander, peppercorns, cloves, allspice, and fennel in a piece of cheesecloth and secure with a piece of kitchen twine to create a flavor purse. Put the purse and the sweet potatoes in a large saucepan and add just enough water to cover. Bring to a boil over medium-high heat and then simmer until the potatoes are soft, 20 to 30 minutes. Drain the potatoes and discard the flavor purse.

In a food mill, food processor, or potato ricer, purée the sweet potato mixture then transfer to a large bowl, add the milk, eggs, sugar, ground ginger, and magic dust, and mash until fully incorporated.

In a large bowl, whisk together the flour, baking powder, and salt. Gradually start adding the sweet potato mixture, stirring well with a wooden spoon until smooth and well combined with no lumps. If you have time, allow the mixture to sit, covered, at room temperature for 2 to 4 hours. While this is not necessary (you could fry immediately if needed), it allows the donut dough to hydrate and the flavors to deepen and bloom.

In a large heavy-bottomed pot over medium-high heat, heat the oil to 350°F on a candy or deep fat thermometer (see frying guidelines, page 45). Line a baking sheet with paper towels and set it near the stove or deep fryer.

Put a large pastry piping bag or resealable plastic bag inside a jar or a spouted measuring cup and roll the top down over the rim of the jar. Carefully add about half of the fritter dough to the bag. Seal or secure the bag if possible and then use scissors to cut a hole about ½ in diagonally across one corner. When the oil reaches 350°F, working in batches, carefully

pipe abstract squiggles of dough into the hot oil and fry, gently flipping with tongs or a slotted spoon, until it's golden brown, about 2 minutes per side. Transfer to the paper towel–lined baking sheet. Pipe and fry the remaining dough, adjusting the heat as needed to keep the oil at 350°F.

TO SERVE: While still hot, drizzle the fritters with the pineapple syrup and sprinkle with more magic dust and powdered sugar. Serve immediately.

CITRUS BLACK SESAME POUND CAKE WITH CHAMOMILE WHIP

Serves 10

Topping

2 cups heavy cream

⅓ cup chamomile
   flowers or 6 bags
   chamomile tea

1 Tbsp confectioners' sugar

1 Tbsp pure vanilla extract
   or vanilla bean paste

2 Tbsp toasted coconut
   flakes (optional)

Cake

1 cup coconut oil, melted
   and cooled but not
   solid, plus more for
   the pan

½ cup unsweetened full-fat
   coconut milk

6 Tbsp Black Sesame Tahini
   (page 197)

1½ tsp activated charcoal

2 cups all-purpose flour,
   plus more for the pan

2 tsp baking powder

1 tsp kosher salt

½ tsp baking soda

3 large eggs, at room
   temperature

1½ cups granulated sugar,
   plus more for sprinkling

2 Tbsp freshly grated lemon
   zest plus 4 tablespoons
   fresh lemon juice (from
   about 1 or 2 lemons)

We love marble in all its forms, especially when it's edible. This recipe takes pound cake to the next level by combining the deep, nutty flavor of black sesame with the light and dreamy flavor of chamomile. This is a casual afternoon cake, but with its marbled and moist interior, it is sure to impress. It makes a great do-ahead birthday cake and lasts for days wrapped or stored in an airtight container. If you aren't going to eat the cake in one sitting, serve the topping on the side for longer storage life.

TO MAKE THE TOPPING: In a small saucepan, combine the heavy cream and chamomile and bring to a simmer over low heat. Continue simmering for 15 minutes then turn off the heat, cover, and let stand for 10 minutes. Pour through a fine-mesh strainer into a bowl; discard any solids. Cover and refrigerate while you make the cake.

TO MAKE THE CAKE: Preheat the oven to 375°F. Brush an 8 by 5 in loaf pan with coconut oil and line the bottom with parchment paper. Brush the parchment with coconut oil then dust the pan with flour, shaking out any excess.

In a large bowl, whisk the coconut milk with ½ cup of water. Set aside.

In a small bowl, combine the black sesame tahini and the activated charcoal and stir vigorously until tahini darkens in color. Set aside until ready to use.

In a medium bowl, whisk together the flour, baking powder, salt, and baking soda.

In the bowl of a stand mixer fitted with the paddle attachment (or in a large bowl with an electric hand mixer set on high), beat the eggs, sugar, and lemon zest until very thick and fluffy, about 5 minutes. With the mixer still running, slowly drizzle in the coconut oil and beat until fully incorporated, about 2 minutes. Reduce the speed to low, and add the coconut-water mixture and the lemon juice. Gradually add the flour mixture and beat until just combined. Transfer half of the batter to a medium bowl. Add ¼ cup of the tahini charcoal mixture and stir until fully incorporated. Set aside the remaining tahini charcoal mixture.

It's marbling time! Place two large dollops of the plain batter in opposite quadrants of the loaf pan. Do the same with the black sesame batter. Using a toothpick or the handle of a spoon, stir the batter to create a marbled effect. Continue layering and swirling until all of the batter is in the pan. Bake until a skewer inserted into the center comes out clean, 45 to 50 minutes. Transfer the cake to a rack to cool for 20 minutes, then run a knife around the edge to release the sides of the cake from the pan. Invert the cake onto a plate and then flip it back over onto the rack. Let cool completely.

While the cake is cooling, finish making the topping. Freeze the bowl of the stand mixer (or large metal bowl if using an electric hand mixer) for 10 minutes. Add the chamomile-infused heavy cream to the bowl and whip until soft peaks form. Add the confectioners' sugar and vanilla and whip until stiff peaks form.

TO SERVE: Use an offset spatula to apply the whipped cream to the top of the cake in undulating waves. Stir the remaining tahini charcoal mixture and, using a spoon, do your best Jackson Pollock impression and splatter the black sauce all over the white whipped cream. Let loose! Sprinkle with the toasted coconut. Enjoy with tea or coffee :)

S'MORES 69: CHARRED MARSHMALLOW WITH CACAO-BUCKWHEAT CHILE CRISP

Serves 1

Cacao-Buckwheat Chile Crisp

2 cups Fragrant Chile Oil
(page 38)
12 garlic cloves, roughly
chopped
One 2 in piece ginger,
peeled and cut into
thin matchsticks
1 shallot, roughly chopped
1 cinnamon stick
1 cup Chile Sludge
(see Fragrant Chile
Oil, page 38)
2 Tbsp cacao nibs
2 Tbsp buckwheat groats
1 tsp granulated sugar

S'more

1 marshmallow
2 bricks Hershey's milk
chocolate
1 graham cracker, broken
into two halves
1 perfect stick (ideally,
foraged from the
woods yourself)

This was the only dessert we had on our Fuego 69 pop-up menu. Because of the pandemic, we could only safely cook and serve food outside. We are hoping that most people out there have experienced the delight of a crispy, gooey s'more around the campfire, but if you haven't, we will break it down for you here. This is really a recipe for the chile crisp, which has a world of different applications beyond this dessert. Enjoy hot off the fire or wrap up and freeze—these bad boys make a great cold treat on a hot day :) You can also drizzle the Cacao-Buckwheat Chile Crisp mixture over anything your heart desires.

TO MAKE THE CACAO-BUCKWHEAT CHILE CRISP: In a small saucepan over low heat, gently bring the chile oil, garlic, ginger, shallot, buckwheat groats, and cinnamon stick to a simmer. Continue gently simmering until the mixture smells fragrant and turns golden brown and crisp, about 20 minutes. Turn off the heat and let cool for a few minutes. Discard the cinnamon stick. Add the chile sludge, cacao nibs, buckwheat groats, and sugar and stir to combine. Use immediately or store in an airtight container in the refrigerator for up to 1 month.

TO MAKE THE S'MORE: We are assuming if you are this far along in the recipe that you are already near a campfire (if not, see How to Make a Fire, page 221). A hot grill will also work, and, for you city kids, a gas range works too, but that seems messy and kind of misses the point.

Find the pointiest part of your stick, the tip if you will, and jab the marshmallow right on it. Position the stick so the marshmallow is directly over the flame. Now there are two types of people in this world, those who slowly and carefully rotate the marshmallow just above the flame, working to achieve a perfect golden-brown color. But that's not us. We prefer to thrust the marshmallow directly into the center of the flame, watching with glee as it blisters and crackles and turns black on all sides. When the marshmallow is about to fall off the stick, remove it from the heat. Arrange the chocolate bricks on a graham cracker half and place the burnt marshmallow on top. Drizzle a generous amount of chile crisp over the marshmallow. Top off with the other graham cracker half. Take a bite.

How to Give Love Advice

When we started as an experimental pop-up restaurant, we loved the idea of having non-food items intermingling with regular appetizers and entrées on our menu. Our first night we had our good friend and local troubadour, Juan Sanchez, offering guests a $5 tableside canción, a passionate Spanish ballad, for dessert—now that's the way to end a meal! We've had soothing warm hand towels in the winter, refreshing rosewater facial spritzes in the summer, and healing herbal tinctures by our local herbalist. But our favorite non-food item has always been love advice. What a way to connect with a stranger!

WHEN DISPENSING LOVE ADVICE, WE WORK WITH A FEW OVERARCHING GUIDELINES:

1. FLEXIBILITY WHEN GIVING LOVE ADVICE IS CRUCIAL: When you give love advice to a stranger, you toe the line between telling them what they *want* to hear and what they *need* to hear. What they need to hear could change as the session progresses, so you may need to adapt.

2. ABANDON THE FOLLOWING:
* the concept of "right" feelings
* the concept of "wrong" feelings
* the concept of "stupid" questions
* any attachment to a specific outcome

3. EMBRACE THESE:
* active questioning and listening
* self-revelation (people feel more comfortable sharing their secrets when you share yours first, but don't overdo it—a few moments of shared anecdotes can go a long way to make someone comfortable)
* fearless honesty and responsiveness to their honesty

And here's how it's done: It's a Friday night, the wait time for two seats at the counter is 45 minutes, and you are sitting down at table 21 with a bachelorette party telling the maid of honor that she might need to break up with her fiancé of five years. She starts to cry, and you start to tear up, too, as you tell her it won't be easy, but from what you're hearing, Mr. Fiancé has a double standard for compromise. He's asking her to quit her job (she's the bigger breadwinner and on her way to becoming a partner). The other problem is that he wants to be in an open relationship for a three-month period when they will be long distance. When you ask her if she wants an open relationship, she falls silent while all members of the bachelorette party say: "No!"

Giving love advice is a big responsibility. For anywhere from two to fifteen minutes, an absolute stranger lets you into their inner world, sharing feelings, insecurities, and personal details about their life. It requires skill and practice to help them feel safe, held, and heard.

The most important practice when giving love advice is to listen without ego. Forget who you are and the way you live your life. Work to understand the person, the situation, and the other players (if there are other players) before bringing your thoughts to the table. Ask questions. Listen for what's not said.

These are rules to live by in both love and life. They will help you connect with strangers as well as your own community.

Acknowledgments ✳ ✳ ✳ Adam + the Yesfolk family, Adam Weinert, Adrienne Hamil, Ale Campos, Alex Guerrero, Alex Patrick Dyck, Alex Wilcox, Alison Roman, Alivia Bloch, Alix+Adrianna, Allison Kizu, Amanda Daisy Lees, Amanda Mummery, Amber Esseiva, Amiel Stanek, Andy Overton, Angela Dimayuga, Angelina Dreem, Anne Alexander & the Cousins gang, Annie Bielski, Anita Otey, Aristilde Kirby, Arley Marks, Audrey Snyder, Azucena, Beth Brown, Betty Studios, Billie Belo, Bradley Vanston, Brett Timothy, Carly "No Cilantro" and Dan, Carmen Macher, Caroline Friedman, Caroline+Darcy, Carver Farrel, Casa Latina Pupusas y Mas, Chaska, Chase & Chaseholm Farms, Checkers, Cherry Iocovozzi, Chinchakriya Un & Ross, Chris, Lucy + the Team at Prix Fixe, Chrissy Rivera, Christine Ripley, Claudia, Coco Gagnet, Common Hands Farm, Dalia Fakhouri, Dan + Tay + the Suarez gang, David Gallardo, Daniel de la Nuez+ Aaron Fox, Davon Rainey, Djuna Schamus, Dove Griffin, effie bowen, Ehm West, Elbert Perez, Elise McMahon, Emily Ritz, Emily Wheeler, Enana Nduku, Inka + Mela, Enky Bayarsaikhan, Erin Gifford, Facundo Huerta, Fifi Essome, Flo Honnet, Francesca Capone + Ryan, Franny+John, Garret McClure, Gerardo Gonzalez, Good Fight Herb Co., Grace Caiazza, The Half Moon Hudson, Hank Flick, Hawkins NY, Ines Gallardo, Ironwood Farm, Izzy New, Jackie Zeller, Jaime Keeling, Jeannette Banashak, Jerry and the Rev gang, Jessanna Britton, Jesse Hart, Jessica Pettway, Jim Wheeler, Jon Wang, Jonathan Osofsky, Jordon Soper, Jori Jayne, Jose Hualca-Gallardo, Juan Sanchez + Lloyda, Judi Powers Jewelry, Julia Johnson, Kamal Johnson, Kasuri, Kate Treacy, Katherine Clary, Kelly Crimmins, The King of Catskill, Kristin Dodge + September Gallery, Ladymoon + the Eclipse, Lauren Giambrone + Good Fight, Lauren Schaeffer, Layla Kaylin, Lee + everyone at Kinderhook Farms, Leisah+Monica, Leor Miller, Letterbox Farm, lexi welch, Liam Turkle, Like Minded Objects, Lila Holland, Linden Crawford, Lisa Usyk, Liz Hopkins, Lizbeth Yeager, Loach Sample, Lou Barnes, Lou our insurance guy, Lucia Hualca-Gallardo, Luka Carter, Lune Wynyard, Mandy Beckley, Mark Bodnar, Mark DePace Material Vodka, Matia Emsellem, Max Taylor-Milner, Merritt Meachem, Mike Mosby, MINNA, Moiety NYC, MOMAPS1, Monica Gallardo, Morningstar Farm, Nathaniel Anschuetz, Ngounga Badila, Nick+Leah+Nialls, Oscar "Stinky" Black-Bodnar, Otis Denner-Kenney, Paige Simpson, parker menzimer, Pati Hertling + everyone at Performance Space, Raphael Wolf, Ray Smith Studio, R.B. Schlather, Ren Cook, Rich Maddocks, Ricky Zoker, Rihanna, Rivertown Lodge, Robin Rose Hill, Roman Horst, La Famila Romero, Rudy Mungaray, Russell Jones Jewelry, Ryan McDermott, Samantha+ Olivia, Sancia Nash, Sara Beckley, Sara Black, Sarah+Nick Suarez and the Gaskins crew, Sean Desiree, Sean Grestley, Sean Roland, September Gallery, Shireen Ahmed, Shanekia McKintosh, Silver Cousler, Sonia Corina, Sophie "Sopho" Biber, Sparrowbush Farm, Tea Boris-Schacter, Ted Levitine-Walsh, Tepper, Tom + Dot, Tomm Roesch, Topless Gallery, Victoria + Peter Gambino, Vanessa Martenson, Victoria Granoff, Vien+Jess+the gang, WGXC Radio, Whistledown Farm, Wyndham Garnett, Yiyi Mendoza, Zack Klug, Zak Pelaccio, Zax Restaurant.

A note on writing this book: We wrote *Please Wait to Be Tasted* in the throes of the pandemic. In most ways, it was the perfect time. No endless days at the restaurant, juggling events and covers and prep lists along with the demands of regular life. We had more time to write, more time to sit with ourselves. In looking back to early 2020, we see the ways that COVID-19 allowed us to look inward, to come to hard realizations, to begin to own our inner truths.

> The team that wrote this book has since chosen to part ways: the trio is no more, though so much love remains. Hannah and Wheeler have both moved on, leaving an incredible legacy behind them, and Carla is honored to have collaborated so closely with them for so long. She is now running the restaurant with a brand-new team. This has been a time for loss, grieving, resistance, and transition. It is with great gratitude for what was, and great hope for what will come, that we now put our energy toward transformation and manifestation and focus on *becoming*.

Thank you

Carla Kaya Perez-Gallardo: A feeling of deep gratitude to my three mothers, present and passed: Inés, Mónica, y Lucía. Ustedes son mis ejemplos más fuertes de cómo compartir amor y comida con una generosidad inmensa. Les agradezco por haberme criado a vivir mi vida sin miedo, y a tener una fé clara y profunda en mi visión para mí misma, y para el mundo que quiero crear.

> A shout-out to the lovers in my life who have seen and supported this project since day one. It's not easy to love someone who is absorbed by passion and focus directed elsewhere. Thank you for giving me room to thrive—and for believing.

And last, but not least, bountiful blooms for my Linden: pillar of support, love, care, clarity, and conversation. Thank you for seeing my shadow side and loving me anyway. Gratitude doesn't begin to describe it—I am humbled to see myself through you, honored for the gift of sight.

> **Hannah Black:** Eternally grateful to all the hands who helped shape this project, especially Mark, who took a wild leap on an artist/chef, held on tight, drove long distances, and stayed up late to make it work: I love you. To Elise, without whom I don't know where I would be living or what I would be doing: thank you for continually lighting that spark and pushing me in the right direction. To Sara, who has always been there to champion the cause, get dirty, work hard, and offer support along this ride: thank you for being there. And finally, to Oscar: loving you is without a doubt the greatest joy I have ever known. Thank you for shaking up everything and transforming my heart.

Wheeler: To my sister, Emily, and my moms, Beth and Jeanette—for reminding me that we are here to take care of each other.

> To Andy, my partner, for teaching me about listening, being brave, and being kind. I love you, thank you.

Works Not Cited

Beehive Design Collective, Mesoamérica Resiste map (beehivecollective.org)

The Cooking Gene: A Journey Through African American Culinary History in the Old South by Michael W. Twitty (Amistad, 2017)

Cruising Utopia: The Then and There of Queer Futurity by José Esteban Muñoz (NYU Press, 2009)

FOOD founded by artists Carol Goodden, Tina Girouard, and Gordon Matta-Clark (SoHo, New York City, 1971)

Infinite City: A San Francisco Atlas by Rebecca Solnit (University of California Press, 2010)

In the Wake: On Blackness and Being by Christina Sharpe (Duke University Press, 2016)

The Wine Bible by Karen MacNeil (Workman, 2015)

You and I Eat the Same: On the Countless Ways Food and Cooking Connect Us to One Another edited by Chris Ying (Artisan, 2018)

Index

Author Biographies

Carla Kaya Perez-Gallardo was raised by three Ecuadorian women in a home with a kitchen that was always busy in Queens, New York. In seventh grade, she started Saborines, a pie company named after her grandmother. After graduating from Bard College with a degree in studio arts, she found a place for herself cooking and managing kitchens. Following a brief pause from cooking and a strained attempt to navigate the traditional art world, she met Hannah Black, and, for the first time, she could imagine a future that celebrated the marriage of art and food.

Hannah Black was born and raised in Alabama, and she attended the Rhode Island School of Design, where she studied painting and also developed a passion for cooking elaborate meals for her community. She has previously worked at Mission Chinese Food in New York City and Hartwood in Tulum, Mexico, before laying down roots in the Hudson Valley.

Wheeler grew up in the Napa Valley, the child of two Presbyterian pastors, and moved to upstate New York to pursue a literature degree at Bard College. While waiting tables to make ends meet, they developed a taste for restaurants and joined the staff of Lil' Deb's Oasis in 2016, at age twenty-two. They served as general manager and wine guy from 2017 to 2021.

From left to right: Carla, Wheeler, and Hannah